IN STEP WITH THE SPIRIT

STUDIES IN THE SPIRIT-FILLED WALK

Denzil R. Miller

IN STEP WITH THE SPIRIT

STUDIES IN THE SPIRIT-FILLED WALK

Denzil R. Miller

AIA Publications
Springfield, Missouri
USA

In Step with the Spirit: Studies in the Spirit-filled Walk

Library of Congress Cataloging-in-Publication Data
Miller, Denzil R., 1946–
In Step with the Spirit: Studies in the Spirit-filled Walk
Denzil R. Miller

ISBN: 978-0-7361-0375-6

1. Pneumatology—Pentecostal. 2. Biblical teaching— 3. Biblical studies—Holy Spirit

Printed in the United States of America
AIA Publications, Springfield, MO, USA
In Step with the Spirit: Studies in the Spirit-filled Walk
03.08/25 ı R/LS/DoDt   CG08EN2570

CONTENTS

INTRODUCTION

The story is told of the mother who was watching a parade of soldiers returning from the war. As the column of soldiers moved by, she saw her son, Johnny, marching proudly with the rest. As he grinned and waved at her, it was painfully obvious that he was out of step with the rest of the soldiers. When everyone else's right foot went forward, Johnny's went backward. When theirs went backward, his went forward. "Would you look at that," the mother exclaimed, "Everyone is out of step except my Johnny!"

The story of Johnny is a parable of many modern Christians. They are out of step, not only with other Christians, but with the Spirit of God. John wrote, "He who has an ear, let him hear what the Spirit says to the churches" (Rev. 2:11). Paul admonished, "Keep in step with the Spirit" (Gal. 5:25). This book will discuss how a believer in Christ may live a life in step with the Spirit of God—one that is lived under the Spirit's guidance and control.

It is my sincere desire that, as a result of reading this book, you will enter into a new and deeper relationship with God the Holy Spirit. Pentecostal scholar Stanley Horton wrote,

> Being born again is not an end in itself. It is only the first step toward living in the Spirit. To the woman at the well Jesus presented himself as the Giver of water that will become in a person a well of water springing up into everlasting life (John 4:10, 14). Thus, He goes beyond the promise of a new birth to

1

the promise of a life in the Spirit, bringing not a few drops of water merely, but a spring or artesian well continually flowing because it comes from a higher source.[1]

This book is meant to be more than just an intellectual exercise. It has been designed as a handbook for a spiritually dynamic life. To receive maximum benefit from this study, it is essential that the reader, once he has encountered a new living truth in these pages, immediately begin to apply that new truth his own spiritual life. It will do little good, for example, if he learns about the baptism in the Holy Spirit and yet fails to be baptized in the Spirit himself. Life in the Spirit is not a thing to be read about and then forgotten; it is rather a life to be experienced and lived daily.

The reader should also note that this book is designed in a special way. The lessons are designed so that they can be used as sermon or teaching outlines. The reader is encouraged to use the lessons in his own preaching and teaching ministry. For example, one chapter could serve as one lesson, or it could be divided and made into two or more lessons. Take, for instance, Chapter 9, "Overcoming Temptation Through the Power of the Spirit." The entire chapter could serve as one lesson, or it can be divided into two complementary lessons, with the first lesson based on the first main point, entitled, "Understanding Our

Temptations" and the second lesson, based on the second main point, entitled "Triumphing Over Temptation."

---

[1] Horton, *What the Bible Says About the Holy Spirit,* (Springfield, MO: Gospel Publishing House, 1976), 115.

It is my hope that you will not only study these lessons and apply them to your own life, but that you will preach and teach them to others.

Denzil R. Miller

Chapter 1

MEET YOUR
REMARKABLE FRIEND

C an two walk together except they be agreed?" So asked the ancient prophet. What is true in the natural realm is also true in the spiritual. Before one can live in step with the Spirit, he or she must first be in agreement with the Spirit. And, before one can be in agreement with the Spirit, he must first come to know the Spirit of God.

The Bible speaks of the "fellowship of the Holy Spirit" (2 Cor. 13:14). This is the blessed privilege of every believer. The Holy Spirit wants to be more to us than just a "doctrine which we believe" or a "tool which we use" to do the work of God. He wants to be our personal Friend and Guide. For this to be, we must learn to live our lives in step with the Spirit. And, in order to live in step with the Spirit, it is essential that we have a clear understanding of just who the Holy Spirit is. In this chapter we will meet our Remarkable Friend—the Spirit of God. We will answer the important question, "Who is the Holy Spirit?"

THE DEITY OF THE HOLY SPIRIT

The Holy Spirit is God

Some conceive the Holy Spirit to be some mysterious power, such as gravity or electricity—or even witchcraft. The Holy Spirit, however, is not such an impersonal force. He is, in fact, God. One writer described the Holy Spirit as "God in action." Throughout Scripture the Holy Spirit is seen performing the works of God.

The Third Person of the Trinity

Sometimes theologians refer to Holy Spirit as the third Person of the Trinity. But what exactly does this mean? In the Bible God is revealed as being a trinity, or tri-unity, of being. This means that, although God is one in His divine essence, He is three in person. He is God the Father, God the Son, and God the Holy Spirit.

Some passages in the Bible speak of God as being one. Deuteronomy 6:4 declares, "Hear, O Israel: The Lord our God is one." Many other passages describe the essential unity of God.[1] And yet, other passages speak of God as being three persons. Paul blessed the Corinthian believers by saying, "May the grace of the Lord Jesus Christ, and the love of God, and the fellowship of the Holy Spirit be with you all" (2 Cor. 13:14). Jesus commanded us to baptize new believers "in the name of the Father, and of the Son, and of the Holy Spirit" (Matt. 28:19).

---

[1] For example see Deut. 4:35, 39; 1 Kings 8:60; Isa. 45:5-6; Mark 12:29-32, John 17:3; 1 Cor. 8:4-6; 1 Tim. 2:5.

These are two of the many references to the Trinity of God in the Bible.[2]

So, just as the Heavenly Father is God; and Jesus, the Son, is God; the Holy Spirit is also God. When we speak of the power of the Holy Spirit we are talking about the power of God. When we talk about the voice of the Holy Spirit we are talking about the voice of God. In fact, anytime we speak about the Holy Spirit we are speaking of God.

All the Attributes of Deity

As God, the Holy Spirit possesses all the attributes, or qualities, of deity. Let's look at four of these divine attributes:

1. He is eternal. As God, the Holy Spirit is eternal. The writer of Hebrews calls Him the "eternal Spirit" (9:14). Being eternal, He has no beginning and no end. He has always been, and He will always be.

2. He is omnipresent. The Holy Spirit is also omnipresent. This means that, as God, He is present everywhere at once. There is no place in all of the universe where the Holy Spirit is not! King David once prayed to God, "Where can I go from your Spirit? Where can I flee from your presence? If I go up to the heavens, you are there; if I make my bed in the depths, you are there"(Ps. 139:7-8).

3. He is omnipotent. Being God, the Holy Spirit is also omnipotent, having all power. The angel announced to Elizabeth, "Nothing is too hard for the Lord" (Luke 1:37). Just think of it:

---

[2] See Gen. 1:1, 26, 11:7; Isa. 48:16; John 14:26; Acts 10:38; Eph. 3:14-16; Heb. 9:14; 1 Pet. 1:2, 3:18, 1 John 3:23-24, Jude 20-21, and Rev. 1:4-5).

when we are filled with the Holy Spirit, we are filled with all of the power of God. Anything that God asks us to do, we can accomplish through His power (1 John 4:4).

4. He is omniscient. The Holy Spirit is also omniscient, that is, all knowing. Paul stated that "the Spirit searches all things, even the deep things of God" (1 Cor. 2:10). Because He is omniscient, the Holy Spirit is never taken by surprise. As we walk in the Spirit, He will reveal to us the things we need to know to do the will of God.

THE PERSON OF THE HOLY SPIRIT

The Holy Spirit is a Person

Having established the fact that the Holy Spirit is God, let's now talk about the fact that He is a person. Some people have no problem conceiving God the Father as a person, and they have no problem conceiving Jesus as a person, but they struggle in conceiving the Holy Spirit as a person. This could be because of His name, the Holy Spirit, sounds like a thing rather than a person.

Paul referred to the Holy Spirit as "the Spirit Himself" (Rom. 8:16, 26)[3] Notice that Paul did not call the Holy Spirit, "the Spirit itself," because He is not a thing, but a divine person. It is always wrong to call the Holy Spirit *it.* We should always refer to the Spirit as *He* or *Him.*

---

[3] The King James Version wrongly translates this phrase as "the Spirit itself." Other translations correct this error.

Like Father, Like Son, Like Spirit

We must never forget that just as God the Father is a person, and God the Son is a person, God the Holy Spirit is also a person. Do not become confused when you hear the Holy Spirit referred to as a person. This does not mean that He is a human being—a physical being like you or me. When we say that the Holy Spirit is a person we are not saying that he is a man or that He has a human body. When we say that He is a person, we are saying that He has a mind and a personality.

Understanding two theological words will help us to better grasp this concept. The first word is *corporeality*. This word means having a body. The other word is *personality*, which means being a person. When we say that the Holy Spirit is a person, we do not mean that He has *corporeality*—a body. What we mean is that he has a mind, emotions, and will, the traits of *personality*.

Listed below are several scriptural references which speak of the personal attributes and activities of the Holy Spirit:

- He has a mind (Rom. 8:27).
- He has a will (1 Cor. 12:11).
- He leads (Gal. 5:18).
- He teaches (John 14:26).
- He convicts (John 16:8).
- He guides (John 16:13).
- He strengthens and encourages (Acts 9:31).
- He helps believers in their weaknesses (Rom. 8:26).
- He intercedes for believers (Rom. 8:26).
- He testifies (Rom. 8:16).
- He restrains (Acts 16:6).

- He can be lied to (Acts 5:3).
- He can be resisted (Acts 7:51).
- He can be blasphemed (Matt. 12:31-32).
- He can be vexed and grieved (Isa. 63:10, Eph. 4:30).

NAMES OF THE HOLY SPIRIT

We can learn much about our Remarkable Friend by studying the names He is given in Scripture. Just as Jesus has many names (i.e., Savior, Lamb of God, the Door, the Way, the Truth, the Life, Lion of Judah, Prince of Peace, and others), and each of these names reveals something about His character and work, so the Holy Spirit has many names, which also reveal something about His character and work. The Spirit is given at least seven major names in the Bible. Let's look briefly at each of these names and their significance.

The Spirit
The Holy Spirit is often referred to as simply "the Spirit." One example is found in 1 Corinthians 2:10, where Paul tells us that "the Spirit searches all things, even the deep things of God." Another example is found in John 3:5, where Jesus talks about being "born of the Spirit." When we use the name Spirit, we remember that He is not limited by a human body. He is all places at all times.

Spirit of God

One of the most common names for the Holy Spirit used in Scripture is "the Spirit of God" (or "the Spirit of the Lord"). Together these two names are used over fifty times in the Bible. The first instance is found in the opening verses of the Bible, where it says that "the Spirit of God was hovering over the waters" (Gen. 1:2). Many other examples can be found in Scripture.[4]

When we call the Holy Spirit the Spirit of God, we are distinguishing Him from all other spirits. He is the Spirit who proceeds from God. He is, as we have said, God Himself.

Holy Spirit

Possibly the Spirit's most common name in the Bible is "the Holy Spirit." King David prayed to God, "Do not cast me from your presence or take your Holy Spirit from me" (Ps. 51:11). Jesus commanded us to baptize new believers "in the name of the Father and of the Son and of the Holy Spirit" (Matt. 28:19).[5]

When we call Him the Holy Spirit we are reminded of His essential nature: He is holy. This means that He is absolutely without sin or evil of any kind. In Romans 1:4 He is called "the Spirit of holiness." He is the one who imparts the holiness of God into the life of the believer (Rom. 8:13; 15:16).

Counselor

---

[4] Judg. 6:34; 1 Sam. 10:10, 16:13-14; Ezek. 11:24; Matt. 3:16; Luke 4:18; Acts 8:39; 1 Cor. 2:14; Eph. 4:30.

[5] Other references include Isa. 63:10-11; Eph. 1:13; 4:30; and 1 Thess. 4: 8.

In His Upper Room Discourse, Jesus four times referred to the Holy Spirit as "the Counselor" (John 14:16, 26; 15:26; 16:7). Here Jesus used the Greek word, *Parakletos.* This word is variously translated, "Comforter," "Helper," or "Advocate." Literally, it means one who walks along side another to help. Jesus said that the Counselor would come and abide with us forever. He is the one who takes the place of Jesus. He will be everything to us that Jesus would be if He were here in person.

Spirit of Christ

The Holy Spirit is also called "the Spirit of Christ." Paul wrote, "If anyone does not have the Spirit of Christ, he does not belong to Christ" (Rom. 8:9). As stated above, the Holy Spirit is the one who comes in Christ's stead. As the Spirit of Christ, He speaks of Christ and reveals Him to the unbeliever (John 15:26); He supplies the faith the unbeliever needs to believe in Christ; then He the imparts the Christ-life to all who believe. Finally, He is the One who makes Christ real in the believer's life.

Holy Spirit of Promise

Paul reminded the Ephesian believers that they had been "sealed with the Holy Spirit of promise" (Eph. 1:13, NKJV). He is the Holy Spirit who has been promised to God's people from ancient times (Joel 2:28-29). In Luke 24:49 and in Acts 1:4 Jesus referred to the baptism in the Holy Spirit as "the promise of the Father" (cf. Acts 2:33).

Spirit of Truth

Four times Jesus called the Holy Spirit "the Spirit of Truth"

(John 14:16-17; 15, 26; 16:13). In these verses Jesus said that the Spirit's work is to live in us, to testify about Jesus, and to guide believers into all truth.

I was once moved very deeply when a missionary colleague of mine looked me in the eye and said, "Of all my friends I consider you my best." In this chapter we have begun to become better acquainted with our Remarkable Friend, the Holy Spirit. We have learned that the He is not an impersonal force but a living Person. He is God in action, the blessed Third Person of the Trinity. His desire is to work in our hearts and help us in every area of our lives. Because the Spirit is a person, He can be known and experienced.

As we continue through this book, we will learn many new and exciting truths about the life the Spirit imparts. We will gain powerful insights into how we may live and walk under the Spirit's oversight. *Get ready to experience your new life in the Spirit!*

CHAPTER 2

LIFE IN THE SPIRIT
ITS BENEFITS AND PREREQUISITES

Recently I was visiting with a friend who is a financial advisor. He was trying to advise me how to best invest some of my retirement savings. He wanted me to receive the maximum return on my investment. It is the same with God. He wants every person to receive the maximum return on his investment in life. This is one reason Jesus came, to give us "life to the full" (John 10:10).

In the last chapter we were introduced to our Remarkable Friend, the Holy Spirit. We learned who He is: He is God, and He is a divine Person. We also learned that we can experience Him and know Him personally. In this chapter we will learn about how we can know God more intimately through living in step with His Spirit. We will examine the benefits and prerequisites for such a life in the Spirit. In doing this, we will seek answers to three important questions: (1) What is meant by the term "in the Spirit?"[1] (2) What are the benefits and blessings of a life lived in step with the Spirit? and (3) What are some prerequisites for living such a life in the Spirit?

Learning the answers to these questions will help us to better understand how we may live a life in step with the Spirit of God.

LIFE IN THE SPIRIT DEFINED

Pentecostal and charismatic Christians often make statements such as this: "He was really in the Spirit when he was ministering today." Or we may accuse, "He was not in the Spirit when he did that!" And yet, there is a problem. While we make such statements, most of us do not clearly understand the true meaning of the biblical phrase "in the Spirit."

What, then, does the term actually mean? In the New Testament the term, or its companion term, "by the Spirit," is used at least twenty-nine times where the word "Spirit" refers to the Spirit of God. In these instances, the term means at least two things: Broadly, it means to be in relationship with the Spirit. In a more specific sense, the term means to be under the influence, control, or guidance of the Spirit of God. Let's look more closely at each of these two definitions.

---

[1] In this book we will often use the two terms "in the Spirit" (which is how the NKJV translates the last part of Galatians 5:25), and "in step with the Spirit" (which is how the NIV translates the same phrase), interchangeably.

In Relationship with the Spirit

To be in the Spirit means to be in relationship with the Spirit. Paul wrote to the Roman Christians, "But you are not in the flesh but in the Spirit, if indeed the Spirit of God dwells in you" (Rom. 8:9). Here the apostle is speaking of a relationship. He says that to be in the Spirit means to be indwelt by the Holy Spirit. We come into this spiritual relationship with God when we are born again by the Spirit of God (John 3:1-7). In this sense all Christians are in the Spirit. Other verses also show that to be in the Spirit means to be in relationship with the Spirit[2]

Under the Influence, Control or Guidance of the Spirit

There is a second meaning of the term in the Spirit. This is the meaning that will most often used in this book. To be in the Spirit means, as we have stated above, to be under the influence, control, or guidance of the Holy Spirit. The phrase is used this way at least twenty times in the Bible. Let's look more closely at this definition by dividing it into two parts:

1. Under the influence of the Spirit. When we say that a person is in the Spirit, we could mean that he is under the influence or control of the Holy Spirit. Six biblical passages clearly demonstrate this truth:

- *Acts 18:5.* Paul was under the Spirit's influence when he was "compelled by the Spirit and testified to the Jews that Jesus is the Christ."

---

[2] cf. Rom. 2:29; Gal. 3:3, and 1 John 3:24.

17

- *Acts 20:22.* On another occasion, Paul again stated that he was "compelled by the Spirit." This time the Spirit was directing him to go to Jerusalem.
- *1 Corinthians 14:2.* In this verse Paul spoke of ministering through spiritual gifts. He said, "For he who speaks in a tongue does not speak to men but to God, for no one understands him; however, in the spirit [or 'by the Spirit'] he speaks mysteries." Here, the apostle equates being in the Spirit with being under the Spirit's influence, as with one speaking in Spirit-inspired tongues.
- *Revelation 1:10.* In this passage John spoke of being under the Spirit's influence when he said, "I was in the Spirit on the Lord's Day."
- *Revelation 4:1-2.* John again testified about being in the Spirit: "After these things I looked, and behold, a door standing open in heaven. And the first voice which I heard was like a trumpet speaking with me, saying, 'Come up here, and I will show you things which must take place after this.' Immediately I was in the Spirit; and behold, a throne set in heaven, and One sat on the throne." This passage says that the Spirit of God came suddenly upon John and seized control of his thought processes. While he was in this state, the Spirit revealed truth to him.
- *Revelation 17:3; 21:10.* In these two passages John was "carried away in the Spirit." He was clearly under the influence of the Spirit.

Upon thoughtfully examining these passages, we can see

that in the New Testament the term *in the Spirit* often means to be under the Spirit's influence or control.

2. *Under the guidance of the Spirit.* The term *in the Spirit* can also mean to be under the guidance of the Holy Spirit. Three passages demonstrate this truth:

- *Luke 2:25-27.* In this passage the Bible says that the Holy Spirit was "upon" the old man Simeon. Then it says that Simeon "came by the Spirit into the temple." Being in the Spirit, he was under the Spirit's guidance.
- *Luke 4:1.* Here the Bible speaks of how Jesus, after being baptized in the Spirt (Luke 3:22), was guided by the Holy Spirit: "Jesus, being filled with the Holy Spirit, returned from the Jordan, and was led by the Spirit into the wilderness" (Luke 4:1). Throughout His ministry Jesus continually walked in the Spirit. As a result He was always guided by the Spirit.
- *Romans 8:14.* In this verse Paul says, "For as many as are led by the Spirit of God, these are sons of God." To be a child of God means that one should walk in the Spirit and be led by Him.

In each of these instances, to be in the Spirit means to be under the leadership or guidance of the Spirit.

As we consider these things, we must remember that this influence of the Spirit of God is not the same for all people and at all times. It can come in different ways and with differing intensities. We must also remember that different Christians may sense and respond to the Spirit's promptings in different ways. Just because we have heard someone testify how he or she was influenced or directed by the Holy Spirit in a certain way, does not necessarily mean that we can expect Him to direct us in exactly the same way. God has a unique way of directing each of us. We should each be open and flexible to His special direction.

In this book, when we talk about life in the Spirit and walking in step with the Spirit, we are talking about a life lived under the Spirit's influence, guidance and control. This is the glorious privilege of every believer. Paul exhorts us, "Since we live by the Spirit, let us keep in step with the Spirit" (Gal. 5:25). This is not an unattainable Christian ideal, it is the norm for the Christian life.

LIFE IN THE SPIRIT, ITS BLESSINGS AND BENEFITS

Great blessings come to the life of the Christian who enters into the wonderful Spirit-filled life. Blessings also come to the church, as more and more Christians learn to walk and live their lives under the Spirit's control. Here are fourteen blessings that come as a result of living a life in the Spirit:

Power to Witness
Possibly the greatest benefit of living a Spirit-filled life is power to witness. Jesus taught that, when a disciple receives the Holy Spirit, he or she receives divine power to witness for Him. He said, "But you will receive power when the Holy Spirit comes upon you; and you will be my witnesses in Jerusalem and in all Judea and Samaria, and to the ends of the earth" (Acts 1:8).

His promise was proven to be true when the disciples

received the Holy Spirit on the Day of Pentecost (Acts 2:1-4). Just weeks before, these same disciples had fled during Jesus' hour of greatest need (Matt. 26:56). They had cowered in a secret room "for fear of the Jews" (John 20:19). However, after receiving the Spirit at Pentecost, they were filled with great boldness. Along with Peter, they stood before the multitudes and witnessed boldly for Jesus (Acts 2:14; 3:12; 4:8, 33).

One of the greatest needs of the church today is people who will witness with boldness and zeal. If we will each be filled with the Spirit, as were these first disciples of Jesus, and if we will learn to walk in the Spirit as they did, then we too will become effective witnesses for Christ. As a result, many will come to the Lord.

Abiding Presence of God

A second benefit of living in the Spirit is that one can experience an abiding presence of God in his or her life. The night before Jesus was to be taken from His disciples and crucified, He gave them some wonderful promises: He told them that He would not leave them as orphans. He said that He would send the Holy Spirit in His place. The Holy Spirit would be "another Helper" for them. All of this would happen when they were filled with the Holy Spirit, whom He would send. He told them that this Heavenly Friend was now with them; however, He would soon be in them (John 14:16-18).

Paul concluded his second letter to the Corinthians with a wonderful prayer of blessing: "The grace of the Lord Jesus Christ, and the love of God, and the fellowship of the Holy Spirit be with you all. Amen" (13:14). Note the phrase "fellowship of the Holy Spirit." The word translated "fellowship" could also be translated "communion." It means a deep, intimate friendship. When Jesus said that the Holy Spirit would be "another Counselor" just like Him, He meant that the Holy Spirit would walk along beside us and help us just as He would if He were here in the flesh.

Divine Guidance

The person who is truly living the Spirit-filled life can also expect the Lord to speak to him and give him guidance. God, through the Holy Spirit, will speak directly to the believer's spirit as He did to Ananias: "So the Lord said to him, 'Arise, and go to the street called Straight'"(Acts 9:11). Today the Spirit-empowered missionary can anticipate the Lord's guidance, just as was received by Paul's missionary party when the Spirit guided them step by step to the country of Macedonia (16:6-10).

Overflowing Joy

The Christian who learns to walk in step with the Spirit will also experience great joy in his or her life. Twice the Bible speaks of the "joy of the Holy Spirit" (Rom. 14:17; 1 Thess. 1:6). One of the fruit of living in the Spirit is joy (Gal. 5:22). So, just as the first Spirit-filled believers "ate their food with gladness and simplicity of heart" (Acts 2:46), so can the one today who has learned the secret of living a life in step with the Spirit.

Power over Satan

Another benefit of living in the Spirit is power over Satan and demons. Jesus promised His disciples, "I give you . . . power over all the power of the enemy, and nothing shall by any means hurt you" (Luke 10:19). This power comes from the indwelling

Spirit. It was by the Spirit of God that Jesus cast out demons (Matt. 12:28). It is through that same Spirit that we can have power over Satan today (1 John 4:4).

A Life of Blessing

Jesus told of a sixth wonderful result of being filled with the Spirit. He said that our lives can become fountains of spiritual life and blessing to others. He said, "If anyone thirsts, let him come to me and drink. He who believes in me, as the Scripture has said, out of his heart will flow rivers of living water" (John 7:37-38).

As a Christian walks in the Spirit, he will have a loving concern for others. This concern will be for both those who are near—that is, in the place where he lives—and those who are afar—that is, in distant lands. Those who come into contact with him will be blessed. They will sense the warm Christ-like spirit coming from that individual. It will be the overflow of the Spirit of God in his life.

Power over Temptation

A seventh benefit of living a life in the Spirit is power over temptation. The Bible promises such power to those who have learned to "walk in the Spirit" (Rom. 8:1-4). Paul said, if we walk in the Spirit we "will not gratify the desires of the sinful nature" (Gal. 5:16). As we learn to "present ourselves to God... as instruments of righteousness," the Bible says we will walk in victory over temptation and sin (Rom. 6:13).

Authentic Worship

An eighth wonderful blessing that comes from living in step

with the Spirit is the ability to enter into authentic worship before God. Jesus told the woman at the well, "God is Spirit" and He must be worshiped "in spirit and in truth" (John 4:24). Jesus Himself "rejoiced in the Holy Spirit" and gave praise to the Father (Luke 10:21). Paul wrote of the Spirit of Adoption who leads us into an intimate relationship with God and causes us to cry out, "Abba, Father" (Rom. 8:15). By living a life in the Spirit we can develop a loving relationship with God. It is out of such a relationship that we become true worshipers of Him.

Spiritual Gifts

Another benefit of living in step with the Spirit is that the Spirit-filled believer can expect to see spiritual gifts manifested in his or her life and ministry. As believers walk in the Spirit, the Lord will release spiritual gifts through them according to His will. As a result, they will bless the church and others. Paul speaks of these manifestations of the Spirit in 1 Corinthians 12:7-10. The release of these gifts should be normal occurrences in believers' lives. They should be anticipated and cherished.

Spiritual Fruit

A tenth benefit of life in the Spirit is spiritual fruit. In Galatians 5:22-23 Paul lists nine "fruit of the Spirit": love, joy, peace, longsuffering, kindness, goodness, faithfulness, gentleness, and self-control. As a believer walks in the Spirit and yields his life to the correction of God's Word, spiritual fruit will begin to develop and grow in his life (John 15:4-5; cf. 14:17, 20).

Deeper Relationship

Another bonus that comes from walking in the Spirit is a

deeper relationship with God. Just as the disciples' relationship with Jesus grew as they spent time in His presence, in the same way, our relationship with God will grow as we spend time walking and living in the Spirit.

Physical Strength and Healing

A twelfth benefit of living a life in step with the Spirit is that the believer can expect to receive physical strength, and even healing, from the hand of God. The Bible speaks of the power of the Holy Spirit to give life to our bodies: "But if the Spirit of Him who raised Jesus from the dead dwells in you, He who raised Christ from the dead will also give life to your mortal bodies through His Spirit who dwells in you" (Rom. 8:11).

According to this verse, the believer can expect three wonderful benefits from God as he walks in the Spirit: He can expect that the Holy Spirit will give strength to his physical body. He can know that the Holy Spirit will bring healing to his

ailing body when he is sick. And he can with hope anticipate the future resurrection of his body.

Prayer Life Strengthened

Another wonderful benefit of the Spirit-filled life is help with our prayers. The disciples once asked Jesus, "Teach us to pray." In response, Jesus taught them, among other things, how to be filled with the Spirit (Luke 11:1-13). We can also expect the Spirit's help when we pray, for the Bible says, "Likewise the Spirit helps in our weaknesses. For we do not know what to pray for as we ought, but the Spirit Himself makes intercession for us with groanings which cannot be uttered" (Rom. 8:26-28). This is one powerful way the Holy Spirit helps us in our prayer lives.

Spiritual Man Renewed

A final benefit of living a life in step with the Spirit is that a person's spiritual man is strengthened and renewed. Paul wrote the Ephesians and spoke of his desire that God would "strengthen [them] with power through his Spirit in [their] inner being" (Eph. 3:16). He further taught that a person who prays in tongues "edifies himself" (1 Cor. 14:4). Jude wrote of two ways in which one builds himself up through prayer in the Holy Spirit. He builds himself up in faith (v. 20) and he keeps himself in the love of God (v. 21; cf. Rom. 5:5).

LIFE IN THE SPIRIT, ITS PREREQUISITES

With so many wonderful benefits accruing, how could anyone not want to learn to live in step with Holy Spirit? There are, however, some things that one must do before he or she can enter into the Spirit-filled life. Let's look at five of those things:

Born of the Spirit

The first prerequisite to living a life in the Spirit is being born again of the Spirit of God. How can one expect to live a life *in the Spirit* if he has never been born *of the Spirit?* Jesus said, "Flesh gives birth to flesh, but the Spirit gives birth to Spirit" (John 3:6). Paul taught that "the man without the Spirit does not accept the things that come from the Spirit of God, for they are foolishness to him, and he cannot understand them because they are spiritually discerned" (1 Cor. 2:14).

Further, Jesus said that "the world cannot accept Him [the Spirit of God] because it neither sees him nor knows him" (John 14:17). It is axiomatic that, before one can understand the things of the Spirit, he must be indwelt by the Spirit.

We are born of the Spirit when we come to God, repent of our sins, and put our complete trust in Christ alone for salvation. As a result, we become new creations in Christ (2 Co 5:17). We become alive to God (Rom. 6:11-13) and to the things of the Spirit of God (John 3:3).

Filled with the Spirit

In addition to being born again by the Spirit of God, the baptism in the Holy Spirit is an essential experience for anyone who desires to live life in step with the Spirit. With this powerful spiritual experience comes power to "be witnesses unto" Christ (Acts 1:8, KJV). Being a witness is broader than witnessing per se. Being a witness involves every area of the Christian life. In addition to being initially baptized in the Spirit, the believer who desires to live life in the Spirit, must also learn to stay full of the Holy Spirit (Eph. 5:18).

Open to the Things of the Spirit

A third requisite to a life in the Spirit is openness to the things of the Spirit. Only those who demonstrate a genuine openness to the Spirit will be able to live in the Spirit. We must never forget that the Spirit of God can be grieved and offended. Like a gentle dove, He will silently depart when our attitudes toward Him are not right. The person who has a closed mind or critical spirit will never be able to live a life in step with the Spirit.

Hunger and Thirst after God

Another requirement for living a life in the Spirit is hunger and thirst after God. Jesus said, "Blessed are those who hunger and thirst for righteousness, for they will be filled" (Matt. 5:6). You may ask, "Filled with what?" Filled with God's righteousness. This righteousness comes from the Spirit of God. To hunger and thirst after righteousness must, therefore, include hungering and thirsting after the Spirit. As we hunger and thirst after the Spirit, we open our hearts to Him and His working in our lives.

Once Jesus cried out, "If anyone is thirsty, let him come to me and drink" (John 7:37). Just as thirst for water draws the deer to a stream, thirst for God will draw us to Christ. As a result, our lives will become like streams of spiritual water flowing out to those around us (vv. 38-39).

Ardently Pursue the Things of the Spirit

A final prerequisite for living the Spirit-filled life is ardent pursuit of the things of the Spirit. Concerning the disciples before they received the Holy Spirit on the Day of Pentecost, the Bible says that "they were continually in the temple praising and blessing God" (Luke. 24:53). After the Day of Pentecost, "every day they continued to meet together in the temple courts" (Acts 2:46). They were ardently pursuing the things of the Spirit. It must be the same with us today. We who would live a life in step with the Spirit must ardently pursue the things of the Spirit of God.

———————

In this chapter we have learned how great blessing comes

28

into the life of the Christian who chooses to live and walk in step with the Spirit of God. In later chapters we will expand on some of the themes we have introduced here. We also learned that, in order to live such a life, the believer must do certain things. Let us not fail to do those things. A life in the Spirit is a life like no other. It is a life filled with blessing and joy. It is the privilege and responsibility of every believer.

CHAPTER 3

THE GATEWAY

TO LIFE IN THE SPIRIT

A vivid recollection of my boyhood is walking through the giant iron gates of a local amusement park. I could hear the organ music blaring in the background. A glorious archway of bright, multi-colored lights spanned the entrance. As I walked wide-eyed into the park, I felt as if I had entered a new world, a world full of excitement and promise. In this chapter we will talk about walking through a gate of true promise—a gate that will lead us into a life in step with the Spirit of God.

In our last chapter we discussed the benefits that come from living a life in step with the Spirit. We also discussed the prerequisites for such a life. One of those prerequisites was the necessity of being filled with, or baptized in, the Holy Spirit. In this chapter we will discuss this baptism in the Holy Spirit and it's relationship to the Spirit-filled life.

Just before Jesus returned to heaven, He gave His disciples a final command: "Do not leave Jerusalem, but wait for the gift my Father promised, which you have heard me speak about. For John baptized with water, but in a few days you will be baptized with the Holy Spirit" (Acts 1:4-5). This spiritual baptism was to be their gateway into the Spirit-filled life.

In this chapter we will answer two questions about this vital Christian experience: What is the baptism in the Holy Spirit? and Why is the baptism in the Holy Spirit so important to a life in the Spirit?

WHAT IS THE BAPTISM IN THE HOLY SPIRIT?

What exactly is this baptism in the Holy Spirit that Jesus spoke about? Scripturally, five things can be said about this experience:

A Biblical Experience

First, the baptism in the Holy Spirit is a *biblical experience.* By this we mean two things: We mean that it has its origin in the Bible, and that it is enjoined upon us by biblical commands. Let's now look at each of these truths in more detail.

1. It has its origin in the Bible. The experience of Spirit baptism is not an invention of man. It is neither the idea of the modern Pentecostal movement nor of any other religious movement. It is found squarely in the pages of the Bible.

Both John the Baptist and Jesus spoke of the baptism in the Holy Spirit. John said, "I baptize you with water for repentance. But after me will come one who is more powerful than I, whose sandals I am not fit to carry. He will baptize you with the Holy Spirit and with fire" (Matt. 3:11). Jesus commanded His disciples, "Do not leave Jerusalem, but wait for the gift my Father promised, which you have heard me speak about. For John baptized with water, but in a few days you will be baptized with the Holy Spirit" (Acts 1:4).

Just before Jesus ascended into heaven, He called His disciples together and spoke of the purpose of this promised experience: "But you will receive power when the Holy Spirit comes on you; and you will be my witnesses in Jerusalem, and in all Judea and Samaria, and to the ends of the earth" (Acts 1: 8). A few days later on the day of Pentecost the disciples were themselves baptized in the Spirit:

> When the day of Pentecost came, they were all together in one place. Suddenly a sound like a blowing of a violent wind came from heaven and filled the whole house where they were sitting. They saw what seemed to be tongues of fire that separated and came to rest on each of them. All of them were filled with the Holy Spirit and began to speak in other tongues as the Spirit enabled them. (Acts 2:1-4)

On that same day Peter declared that the experience is for all of God's people throughout the entire church age: "The promise is for you and your children and for all who are far off—for all whom the Lord our God will call" (Acts 2:39).

2. It is enjoined by biblical commands. Not only does the experience have its origin in Scripture, in addition, all believers are commanded to receive the Holy Spirit. Before He returned to heaven Jesus gave His disciples a final promise and a final command. The promise was, "I am going to send you what my Father has promised." The command was, "Stay in the city until you have been clothed with power from on high" (Luke 24:49). He repeated His command: "Do not leave Jerusalem, but wait for the gift my Father promised" (Acts 1:4). Some twenty-five years later, Paul commanded the Ephesian believers, "Be filled with the Spirit" (Eph. 5:18).

Every believer in Christ is under divine obligation to be filled with the Spirit. To do otherwise is to live in direct disobedience to the clear command of the Lord. The baptism in the Holy Spirit is clearly a biblical experience. It has its origin in the experience of the New Testament church, and it is enjoined upon all believers of all ages.

A Distinct Experience

Not only is the baptism in the Holy Spirit a biblical experience, it is also a distinct experience. By this we mean that the baptism in the Holy Spirit is an experience separate from and in addition to the new birth. This fact is clearly demonstrated in the book of Acts. On three separate occasions in Acts it is shown that the new birth and the baptism in the Holy Spirit are separate and distinct experiences. Let's look briefly at each of those three occasions:

1. The revival in Samaria (Acts 8:4-17). A thoughtful reading of the story of the revival that came to Samaria under the ministry of Philip shows that the Samaritan converts were first saved, then later received the Holy Spirit. We know that they were truly saved because

- *they had received the message of Christ.* Acts 8:6 states that the Samaritans "heeded the things spoken by Philip" (NKJV).

- *they experienced great joy.* As a result of their receiving the message of the gospel "there was great joy in the

34

city" (v. 8).

- *they believed and were baptized in water.* "But when they believed Philip as he preached the good news of the kingdom of God and the name of Jesus Christ, they were baptized both men and women" (v. 12). Philip, a man full of the Holy Spirit and wisdom (Acts 6:3) would have never allowed these new believers to be baptized in water if they had not been truly born again.

And yet, it is very clear that they had not yet received the Holy Spirit (in the sense of Spirit baptism) for the text says, "The Holy Spirit had not yet come upon any of them; they had simply been baptized into the name of the Lord Jesus" (v. 16). Only later did they receive the Spirit: "Then Peter and John placed their hands on them, and they received the Holy Spirit" (v. 17).

There is a clear time lapse between the Samaritans' receiving Christ and their receiving the Holy Spirit. We conclude that their new birth and their Spirit baptism are separate and distinct experiences.

2. Saul of Tarsus (Acts 9:1-19). Saul of Tarsus (later called Paul) was converted on the Damascus road, and was later filled with the Spirit when Ananias prayed for him in the city of Damascus. We know that he was truly converted when he encountered Jesus on the road because

- *he called Jesus "Lord"* (v 5). Paul himself wrote that "no one can say, 'Jesus is Lord,' except by the Holy Spirit" (1 Cor. 12:3). At this moment, as Saul of Tarsus lay on the ground before the resurrected Christ, Jesus became his Savior and the Lord.

- *he obeyed Jesus and submitted to His will* (vv. 6-9). One proof of a person's being truly born again is submission to the will of Christ. Jesus commanded Saul to go into the city of Damascus to receive further instructions. Though he was now blind, Saul submitted himself totally to the will of his newly-found Savior and followed His instructions explicitly.

- *Ananias called him "Brother Saul"* (v. 17; cf. Acts 22:13). Ananias called Saul "brother" because he realized that he had become a member of the brotherhood of believers, the Church. Howard Ervin wrote,

> From the preceding context, it is clear that Ananias knew who Saul was and why he had come to Damascus—to persecute the believers there. He would never, therefore, have entered Saul's presence and addressed him as "Brother Saul," unless he had been assured in advance that Saul was, in very truth a "Brother" in Christ. Saul must, therefore have become a Christian, in the fullest sense of the word, before Ananias came to him.[1]

It was sometime after Saul became a Christian that Ananias placed his hands on him, and Saul received the Holy Spirit (vv. 17-18). Again, as in the case of the Samaritan believers, Saul's experience of being filled with the Spirit was subsequent to and separate from his new birth.

  3. The Ephesian disciples (Acts 19:1-7). The twelve

---

[1] Howard M. Ervin, *Spirit Baptism, a Biblical Investigation* (Peabody, MA: Hendrickson Publishers, 1987), 76.

Ephesian disciples were saved and baptized in water, and then later filled with the Spirit when Paul laid his hands on them. The fact that they were truly converted is demonstrated by the following:

- *They are called disciples.* The Bible says when Paul arrived at Ephesus "he found some disciples" (v. 1). Without exception, when the word disciple is used by Luke (the writer of the gospel of Luke and Acts) without any modifying words (such as "disciples of John" or "disciples of the Pharisees") it always refers to disciples of Christ. These men were clearly believers in and followers of Jesus.
- *They had already believed in Christ.* The text clearly states that these men had believed the message of John the Baptist concerning Jesus and had put their faith in Him (v. 4).
- *They were baptized in water.* According to verse 5, "They were baptized into the name of the Lord Jesus." Even if, as some contend, these disciples were not truly converted when Paul found them, certainly they must have been converted before they received water baptism.

After this Paul laid hands on them, and "the Holy Spirit came on them, and they spoke in tongues and prophesied" (v. 6). Like the Samaritans and Saul before them, the Ephesians' experience of Spirit baptism was subsequent to and separate from their new birth.

Having examined these three cases in the book of Acts, we conclude that the baptism in the Holy Spirit is an experience distinct from the new birth.

A Normative Experience

A third thing that we can say about the baptism in the Holy Spirit is that it is a normative experience. By this we mean that it is an experience for all of God's children of all ages and of all cultures. This fact is demonstrated by what Dr. Lazarus M. Chakwera, President of the Malawi Assemblies of God, called the "Alls of Pentecost":

- *Moses' wish for all of the Lord's people.* When Joshua wanted Eldad and Medad to stop prophesying in the camp, Moses replied, "I wish that all of the Lord's people were prophets, and the Lord would put his Spirit on them!" (Num. 11:29).
- *Joel's prophecy concerning all of God's servants.* God spoke through the ancient prophet, "Afterward, I will pour out my Spirit on all people. Your sons and your daughters will prophesy, your old men will dream dreams, your young men will see visions. Even on my servants, both men and women, I will pour out my Spirit in those days (Joel 2:28-29).

- *The Spirit's filling all on the Day of Pentecost.* When God poured His Spirit on the Day of Pentecost "all of them were filled with the Holy Spirit . . ." (Acts 2:4).
- *All of the household of Cornelius received.* The Spirit was first poured out on Gentiles believers in Caesarea at the house of the Roman centurion, Cornelius. The Bible

says that "the Holy Spirit came on all who heard the message" (Acts 10:44-47).

After the outpouring of the Spirit on the Day of Pentecost, Peter stood to preach. He quoted the prophesy of Joel, saying that God would pour out His Spirit on "all people" (Acts 2:17). He concluded his sermon by saying, "The promise is for you and your children and for all who are far off—for all whom the Lord our God will call" (v. 39).

The promise of the Spirit's empowering is a universal promise for all of God's children. Jesus said that this experience is for everyone who asks: "Ask and it will be given to you . . . For everyone who asks receives . . . If you then, though you are evil, know how to give good gifts to your children, how much more will your Father in heaven give the Holy Spirit to those who ask him (Luke 11: 9-10,13).

A Powerful Experience

The baptism in the Spirit is a powerful life-changing experience. Jesus said that the Holy Spirit would come upon the believer as "power from on high" (Luke 24:49). When a believer is filled with the Spirit he or she is immersed in and overcome by God's mighty power and presence. Once a person is truly baptized in the Holy Spirit, his or her life will never be the same. J. Rodman Williams describes the experience as "an invasion from without . . . and a penetration, a permeation" within the heart of the believer. He further describes it as the coming of "the dynamic presence of God" and a manifestation of God's glory.[2]

Spirit baptism was a powerful life-changing experience for Peter and the others who were filled with the Spirit in the book of Acts. Their lives were dramatically and permanently altered. Today, millions of people around the world can testify to the powerful effects this experience has had on their lives.

A Necessary Experience

Finally, the baptism in the Holy Spirit is a necessary experience. It is essential that every Christian be baptized in the Holy Spirit. Just as Jesus insisted that His disciples not leave Jerusalem until they were clothed with the Spirit (Luke 24:49; Acts 1:4-5), so must we insist on every Christian being filled with the Spirit today. It is the believer's source of spiritual life and power. It is the gateway into the Spirit-filled life of which we are speaking in this book.

Reader, have you been baptized in the Holy Spirit? If not, you should carefully read the following chapter, and then ask God to give you this blessed experience. Don't try to live your Christian life without it. Pastor, do you have church members who have never received the Holy Spirit? Then one of your primary ministry goals must be to see that every member in your congregation is wonderfully filled with the Spirit and living the Spirit-filled life.

WHY IS THE BAPTISM IN THE HOLY

---

[2] J. Rodman Williams, *Renewal Theology*, II (Grand Rapids: Zondervan Publishing House, 1990), 203-204.

SPIRIT SO IMPORTANT TO A LIFE IN THE SPIRIT?

Someone may ask, "Why this emphasis on the baptism in the Holy Spirit? Why should I be filled? What are some of the benefits that I can expect by being filled with the Spirit?" The baptism in the Holy Spirit will bring the following four benefits into the life of the believer who receives:

Greater Effectiveness

Being filled with the Spirit opens the way for greater effectiveness in the work of the Lord. The experience will empower the believer for effective service in three primary areas of his or her Christian life:

1. Power to witness. Power to witness comes with the infilling of the Spirit. Jesus promised, "You will receive power when the Holy spirit comes on you; and you will be my witnesses" (Acts 1:8). This power to witnesses involves both motivation and ability. When a person is filled with the Spirit he receives great motivation to become actively involved in the work of the Lord. Not only is he motivated to work for the Lord, he is also enabled to work for Him. This enabling is for both local evangelism and world missions, for Jesus said we would be

witnesses in "Jerusalem and all Judea and Samaria and to the ends of the earth" (Acts 1:8).

2. Power in prayer. An effective prayer life is a must for every believer. Several times in the book of Acts the Holy Spirit came upon Spirit-baptized believers enabling them to pray with great power and effectiveness. After the Day of Pentecost the newly Spirit-baptized believers "devoted themselves . . . to prayer" (2:42). Peter and John are seen "going up to the temple at the time of prayer" (3:1). On one occasion there was a powerful Spirit-anointed prayer meeting that ended with over five thousand people being filled or refilled with the Spirit (4:23-31; cf. 4:4). During the same prayer meeting their meeting place was shaken by the power of God. Today, those who have been filled with the Spirit testify to a greater freedom, effectiveness, and power in their prayer lives and in their ministries.

3. Manifestation of spiritual gifts. Spiritual gifts are given to Spirit-filled Christians to enable them to effectively accomplish the will of God. Since the gifts of the Spirit are resident in the Spirit, and the Spirit is powerfully resident in those who have been baptized in the Holy Spirit, one can logically expect the manifestation of spiritual gifts in the lives of these Christians. In 1 Corinthians 12:8-10 Paul lists nine powerful spiritual gifts. He calls them "manifestations" of the Spirit (v. 7). Around the world Spirit-baptized believers are ministering in the power and anointing of the Spirit with the aid of these mighty spiritual manifestations.

Spiritual Sensitivity

Not only will the baptism in the Holy Spirit empower the Christian for effective service, it will also enable him or her to live a life that is more sensitive to the things of God. This spiritually sensitive life can be seen in at least three areas:

1. Sensitivity to sin, righteousness, and judgment. Jesus said, "When he [the Counselor] comes, he will convict the world of guilt in regard to sin and righteousness and judgment" (John 16: 8). The Spirit-filled believer will have a greater sensitivity to the sin in his own life. Once he has been baptized in the Spirit, and learns to walk in the Spirit, he will be more keenly aware of the slightest personal transgression or departure from God's will. He will have a desire to live a holy life and please God in everything he does.

2. *Sensitivity to God.* The Spirit-baptized believer will also be more sensitive to God and His working in his life. Paul testified, "We have not received the spirit of the world, but the Spirit who is from God, that we may understand what God has freely given us" (1 Cor. 2:12). The person who is filled with, and walking in, the Spirit will be able to more clearly sense the indwelling presence of God in his own life, as well as the Spirit's presence in the life of others (Rom. 8:16).

3. *Sensitivity to the spiritual needs of others.* Once a Christian has been filled with the Spirit, he will find himself more sensitive to the spiritual needs of others. At times the Spirit will help him to see deep into the hearts and needs of hurting people. This was what often happened to Jesus. The Bible says about Jesus, "When he saw the crowds, he had compassion on them, because they were harassed and helpless, like sheep without a shepherd" (Matt. 9:36). The Holy Spirit will also give to us such spiritual sensitivity to the needs of others.

Spiritual Understanding

A third benefit of being filled with the Holy Spirit is a greater potential for spiritual understanding. This greater understanding can be seen in three areas:

1. *Greater understanding of the Word.* Once a person is

filled with the Spirit he or she will have greater insight into Scripture. Paul said, "The man without the Spirit does not accept the things that come from the Spirit of God, for they are foolishness to him, and he cannot understand them, because they are spiritually discerned" (1 Cor. 2:14).

Without the Spirit's help we cannot understand those things which come from the Spirit. We know that the Bible comes from the Spirit of God (2 Pet. 1:21). We must, therefore, have the Spirit to truly understand the Word of God. Jesus said that "when he, the Spirit of truth, comes, he will guide you into all truth" (John 16:13). The Holy Spirit will lead us into a keener and more intimate understanding of God's Word.

2. *Greater understanding of the moving of the Holy Spirit.* The Spirit is moving in the world today. In some places His moving is bringing about a great harvest of souls. In other places He is preparing the soil for the sowing of the gospel. Speaking figuratively about the Holy Spirit Jesus said, "The wind blows wherever it pleases. You hear its sound, but you cannot tell where it comes from or where it is going. So it is with everyone born of the Spirit" (John 3:8). The Spirit is moving in the world, and the person who is filled with the Spirit can have divine insight on what He is doing. Such insight is essential if we are going to fulfill Christ's mandate to preach the gospel to all nations before He comes again (Matt. 24:14).

3. *Greater understanding of the needs of the church and society.* The Bible says concerning certain of David's men that they "understood the times and knew what Israel should do" (1 Chron. 12:32). These were men of clear spiritual insight. The Holy Spirit can give such clear prophetic insight to the needs of His people today. Six times in Revelation, chapters 2 and 3, the

reader is exhorted to "hear what the Spirit says the churches."
Two key questions for us today are, "What is the Spirit saying to
the Church?" and "How is He moving in society?" We must be
filled with the Spirit to be able to clearly discern either.

Deeper Love and Consecration

A fourth result of being baptized in the Holy Spirit is a
deeper love for and consecration to God. Paul wrote that "God
has poured out his love into our hearts by the Holy Spirit, whom
he has given us" (Rom. 5: 5). Being filled with the Holy Spirit
will produce a deeper love and consecration in the life of the
believer. He will experience this deeper love and consecration in
at least three areas of his life:

*1. Deeper love for Christ and a consecration to serve Him
more perfectly.* The Spirit-filled believer's love for Christ will
grow as he walks with the Spirit. Jesus told us that "when the
Counselor comes . . . he will testify about me" (John 15:26). He
also said that "He will bring glory to me by taking from what is
mine and making it known to you" (16:14). As we come to know
Christ more intimately, we love Him more deeply. As we come
to love Him more deeply, we are inspired to serve Him more
perfectly.

*2. Deeper love for the Word and consecration to obey it
more fully.* Not only does the infilling of the Holy Spirit bring
about a deeper love for Christ, it also brings about a deeper love
for the Word of God. As the Spirit-filled Christian becomes
better acquainted with the Author of the Bible, the Holy Spirit,
he will love the Bible more.

Once a young lady was given a book of love poems. After
reading one or two of the poems, she became bored and placed

the book on her shelf. After some time she met a young man and fell and love with him. She soon learned that he was the very poet who had written the book of poems that she had placed on her shelf. She again took up the book and began to read. This time her heart was thrilled as each poem spoke directly to her innermost being. The book of poems now became her most cherished possession. She had fallen in love with the author, and now she loved the book.

The same thing will happen with the Bible. As you grow to love the Author more and more, you will also grow to love the Book He wrote. The Author of the Bible, the Holy Spirit, will make its stories more vivid and its truths more precious. It will become a delight to follow its teachings.

3. Deeper love for the lost and consecration to pursue them more ardently. Not only will the infilling of the Spirit cause the believer to love Christ and the Word more deeply, it will also cause him to have a deeper love for the lost and a greater commitment to reach them for Christ. When the Holy Spirit pours God's love into our hearts, it will include His love for the lost people of the world. Jesus told us to lift up our eyes "and look at the fields! They are ripe for harvest" (John 4:35). We must pray, "Holy Spirit, fill me today. Open my eyes to see the lost as Jesus sees them, and give me the consecration to reach out to them as He did."

If the baptism in the Holy Spirit will bring such blessings into the life of the Christian, who would not want this blessed experience? Reader, have you been filled with the Spirit? If not, you can be today. Carefully read the next chapter, and then ask

God to baptize you in the Holy Spirit today. A wonderful life in the Spirit awaits you, a life lived in step with the Spirit of God.

CHAPTER 4

YOU CAN BE FILLED
WITH THE HOLY SPIRIT TODAY

The old adage says, "The proof of the pudding is in the tasting." The ancient Psalmist once cried out, "Taste and see that the Lord is good" (Ps. 34:8). The issue that every sincere follower of Christ must face is not simply knowing about the blessings of the Spirit-empowered life, the issue is experiencing them.

In our last chapter we discussed how the baptism in the Holy Spirit is the gateway into the Spirit-filled life. We spoke of the blessings that come into a believers life as a result of receiving the Spirit. In this chapter we will discuss how a person can have this wonderful experience. Acts 2 describes the first time the gift was given:

> When the day of Pentecost came they were all together in one place. Suddenly a sound like the blowing of a violent wind came from heaven and filled the whole house where they were sitting. They saw what seemed to be tongues of fire that separated and came to rest on each of them. All of them were filled with the Holy Spirit and began to speak in other tongues as the Spirit enabled them. (Acts 2: 1-4)

The experience of the believers on the day of Pentecost set the pattern for God's people until Jesus comes again. This wonderful gift that was given to those early believers is promised to all believers of all generations. On the same day, Peter told the people gathered there, "The promise is for you and your children and for all who are far off—for all whom the Lord our God will call" (Acts 2:39).

In this chapter we will talk about how you, and those to whom you minister, can receive the gift of the Holy Spirit. We will discuss four issues concerning receiving Spirit baptism: (1) the elements involved in receiving the Spirit, (2) four things one needs to know when he or she comes to be filled with the Spirit, (3) five common misunderstandings concerning receiving the Spirit, and (4) what one must do to be filled with the Spirit. As you read this chapter, open your heart to God. Allow the Holy Spirit to fill and empower you, just as He did those first disciples on the Day of Pentecost.

ELEMENTS INVOLVED IN RECEIVING THE SPIRIT

Whether one is wanting to be filled with the Spirit himself, or he is seeking to lead others into the experience, it is helpful to know what is involved in the experience. Scripturally, there are five essential elements involved in one's receiving the Holy Spirit. Let's look briefly at each:

Desiring the Spirit

Before one can be filled with the Spirit, he or she must first have a desire for the Spirit. He must sincerely want a closer walk with God, and must have a desire to be more useful in His kingdom. God will not force this experience on anyone. Speaking about the Holy Spirit, Jesus said, "Seek and you will find; knock and the door will be opened unto you" (Luke 11:9, cf. v. 13). Seeking and knocking imply strong desire.

Desire for the Spirit can be created in a person's heart in many ways. He may hear a sermon or a teaching on the subject. He may see how the experience has blessed the lives of others. A hunger may be created as he talks with Spirit-filled friends. And yet, although desire my be created in a number of ways, ultimately it must come from within the heart of the individual. Jesus was speaking of the Spirit-filled life when He said, "Out of his heart [innermost being] will flow rivers of living water" (John 7:38). Being filled with the Spirit begins on the inside, with a heart that is hungry for more of God.

Asking for the Spirit

A second essential element in receiving the Spirit is asking. The Bible says, "You do not have because you do not ask" (James 4:2). This principle can be applied to receiving the Holy Spirit. One must ask in order to receive. Speaking of the Holy Spirit, Jesus said, "Ask and it will be given to you . . . everyone who asks receives . . . your heavenly Father [will] give the Holy Spirit to those who ask Him!" (Luke 11:9, 10, 13).

It is God's desire that everyone of His children be filled with the Spirit. He is not withholding His blessing. He is patiently waiting for us to ask. Will you ask Him now? He will give you the Holy Spirit today.

Exercising Faith

A third essential element for receiving the Holy Spirit is faith. Jesus said that this experience is for "he who believes" (John 7:38). Paul taught that the promise of the Spirit is received by "believing the message" (Gal. 3:2, 5, 14).

The Holy Spirit is received by an act of confident faith. Jesus said, "Whatever you ask for in prayer, believe that you have received it, and it will be yours" (Mark 11:24). This general principle of believing prayer has a direct application to asking for and receiving the Holy Spirit. Notice how, in this promise, Jesus put faith in the immediate present tense. He does not say "believe that you *will* receive," but "believe that you *have* received." Faith is the primary ingredient for receiving the Spirit. Just believe that you *have* received the Holy Spirit, and the experience will be yours!

Receiving

Closely akin to faith is the act of receiving, as mentioned above. This is the fourth element involved in being filled with the Holy Spirit. Receiving the Holy Spirit cannot be a passive act. We cannot simply wait passively on God to fill us. We must act with boldness. We must fearlessly reach out and take what God is offering. The Bible teaches that, because of the work of Jesus on the cross, we can enter into the presence of God with confidence (Heb. 10:19). Don't wait for God to force His Spirit upon you; He will never do that. And yet, His hand is already outstretched, He is waiting for you to take the gift from Him. Claim the fullness of the Spirit right now by the bold act of receiving.

Speaking

A final essential element involved in receiving the Holy Spirit is speaking. The Bible says that on the day of Pentecost "they were all filled with the Holy Spirit *and began to speak...*" (Acts 2:4, italics added). As they spoke, the Holy Spirit performed a miracle in their mouths, and they began to speak "with other tongues as the Spirit gave them utterance." What were they speaking? It was "the wonderful works of God" in the languages of the surrounding Gentile nations (v. 11). Much the same thing happened in Caesarea at the home of Cornelius where the Jewish Christians "heard them speaking in tongues and praising God" (Acts 10:46).

Once you have, by an act of faith, received the Holy Spirit, you will sense His presence deep within. You should then begin to boldly speak out, allowing the Spirit to take control and pray through you. You will begin speaking in a beautiful new language. The language will not come from your mind, but from deep inside your inner man. Jesus said, "He who believes in Me, as the Scripture said, 'From his innermost being will flow rivers of living water'" (John 7:38, NASB).

WHAT YOU NEED TO KNOW WHEN YOU COME TO BE FILLED WITH THE SPIRIT

When one comes to be filled with the Spirit, it is helpful to have a proper understanding of certain biblical truths. There are four truths one needs to understand when he presents himself to God to be filled with the Spirit. Let's look at each of these truths:

If You Are Saved, You Are Ready

The first truth one needs to understand when he comes to receive the Holy Spirit is that, if he is born again, he is ready now to be filled with the Spirit. There are no other preconditions. If one has truly put his faith in Christ and repented of his sins (Acts 2:38), then he has obeyed God (5:32), and God is ready now to give him His Holy Spirit.

Many years ago, when I was seeking to be filled with the Spirit, I was told by a sincere but misinformed friend, "You're not being filled because you're not yet holy enough. The Holy Spirit will not enter into an unclean temple." I learned later that this was not sound scriptural advice. Certainly, God expects us to live clean and holy lives, and we must constantly search our lives and repent of anything that displeases God. My friend was right about that, but the fact is, if a person's temple (i.e., his body) is clean enough for Jesus to dwell in, it is clean enough for the Holy Spirit to fill.

If you are truly saved, you are ready right now to receive the Holy Spirit. If you will receive Him, He will give you the

54

power you need to overcome your struggles with temptation and sin.

Being Filled Is Easy

A second thing one needs to know when coming to be filled with the Spirit is that receiving the Spirit is not difficult. Some people have the idea that being filled with the Holy Spirit is very difficult, and requires much agonizing and pain. But this is not what the Scriptures teach. The Bible teaches that we receive the Spirit by simply asking in faith (Luke 11:9-13; cf. Mark 11:24). It teaches that God is ready to give His Spirit to those who will ask. Being filled with the Spirit is not something abnormal or out of the ordinary for the born again believer; it is the natural thing to do.

Once Jesus related receiving the Holy Spirit to breathing: "And when He had said this, He breathed on them, and said to them, 'Receive the Holy Spirit'" (John 20:22). Receiving the Spirit is to our spiritual man as normal as breathing is to our natural man. It should never be thought of as being difficult.

Remember, when a believer comes to be filled with the Spirit, he is not seeking to be filled with *another* Holy Spirit. He is seeking to be filled with the same Holy Spirit who already indwells him. He is the same Spirit who entered his life when he was born again (John 3:5; Rom. 8:9). A man once said, "When you were born again, you 'breathed in' the Holy Spirit. Now, just take a deeper breath and be filled with the Spirit." What a beautiful thought. Being filled with the Spirit is as simple as asking, believing, and receiving.

Leave Your Pride Behind

55

A third truth we must understand when we come to be baptized in the Spirit is that we must leave all pride and vanity behind. Such things have no place in our walk with God. They are the very things that hinder some from being filled with the Spirit. The Bible says, "God opposes the proud but gives grace to the humble" (1 Pet. 5:5).

Some are proud of their position in the church and, therefore, will not admit they need to be filled with the Spirit. Others fear what people will say when they present themselves to be filled with the Spirit. Still others fear looking foolish. My friend, put your pride behind you. Humble yourself before God and be filled with the Spirit today.

Expect to Speak in Tongues

The person seeking the empowering of the Spirit should also know that when he is baptized in the Holy Spirit, he will speak in other tongues as the Spirit gives utterance. Everyone who comes to be filled with the Spirit should, therefore, expect to speak in tongues as a sign of his being filled. This was the recurring Scriptural evidence throughout the book of Acts.

At Pentecost the believers "began to speak in other tongues as the Spirit enabled them" (Acts 2:4). At the house of Cornelius the Gentile believers were heard "speaking in tongues and praising God" (10:46). Years later the Ephesian disciples "spoke in tongues and prophesied" (19:6). Today millions of people around the world have received this same experience with the same biblical evidence. It has been my great privilege to pray with thousands of hungry believers across Africa and see them empowered by the Holy Spirit as were those believers in the book of Acts—and with the same biblical evidence. They wonderfully spoke in tongues as the Spirit gave them utterance!

COMMON MISUNDERSTANDINGS CONCERNING RECEIVING THE SPIRIT

Some are hindered from receiving the Holy Spirit because of certain misunderstandings they have concerning how He is received. For these people, the answer to their problem is to simply clear up of these misunderstandings. Once this happens, they are happily filled with the Spirit. There are five common misunderstandings which hinder people from being filled with the Spirit:

Passively Waiting on God

Some have a misunderstanding about how God gives His Holy Spirit. They have wrongly interpreted the passages that speak of how the Holy Spirit is poured out on believers (Acts 2:17-18, 33; 10:45). As a result, they passively wait on the Holy Spirit to come suddenly and irresistibly upon them and "do it to them." They are like the man who once said, "God knows my address. If He wants to fill me with the Spirit, He knows where He can find me."

This is the wrong attitude for receiving the Holy Spirit. While it is true that the Spirit is poured out afresh on believers today, we must understand that He is poured out in response to our active faith in Him. We ask in faith, He then pours out His Spirit on us.

Once a man was having difficulty being filled with the Spirit. He was passively waiting on God to pour out His Spirit on him. His pastor was trying to explain to him how he must take the initiative and, by faith, receive the Spirit. Then the pastor remembered that this man loved to play checkers,[1] so he asked him a question, "My friend, suppose you are playing a game of checkers. You have moved your piece. Now, what must happen before you can move again?" The man answered, "Of course, the other man must move." Then the preacher said, "God has moved. He has already poured out His Spirit. Now, it is your move. Before God can move again, and give you the Holy Spirit, you must move in faith and ask Him to fill you." The man then reached out in faith and God filled him with the Holy Spirit.

Looking for the Spirit to Fall from Above

There is another misunderstanding common among people seeking to be filled with the Holy Spirit. These people are looking for the Holy Spirit to come down from heaven, smack them on top of the head, overpower them, and begin speaking through them.

This is not how the Holy Spirit is received. He will not fall on your head from above, but He will fill you from the inside. He will rise up within you, and gush forth from inside you. Jesus described being filled with the Spirit like this:

> If anyone is thirsty, let him come to me and drink. Whoever believes in me, as the Scripture has said, streams of living water will flow from within him. By this he meant the Spirit,

---

[1] Checkers is the American name for the British game of draughts.

whom those who believed in him were later to receive. (John 7:37-39)

When you come to be filled with the Spirit, don't expect Him to fall on your head from above. Look for Him to rise up within you. You will sense Him moving inside. When you sense His fullness within, you know that He has come to fill you. At that moment "believe that you have received" and boldly speak out in faith. Let the rivers of living water flow!

Thinking That God Is Going to Impose Tongues

There is a third common misunderstanding about receiving the Spirit. Some seekers believe that at some point while they are praying in their own language, or not praying at all, God is going to forcibly take over their vocal chords and speak through them. But this will never happen. God will not force the Holy Spirit upon anyone. Neither will He force anyone to speak in tongues. On they Day of Pentecost "they [the 120 believers] began to speak in tongues." It was the believers who were speaking, but it was the Spirit who "enabled them" (Acts 2:4).

Remember, you will speak. It will be your lungs, your vocal chords, your lips, and your tongue creating the sounds. It will be you speaking, but it will be God who will give you the words. The miracle is not the speaking; the miracle is the new language. You must speak forth in faith, trusting God to fill your mouth.

Being Focused on Speaking in Tongues

A fourth common mistake made by some seeking to be baptized in the Spirit is that they become more focused on speaking in tongues than on experiencing the presence and power of God. Most people who come to be filled with the Spirit know that they will speak in tongues. This is good; however, some become so intent on trying to speak in tongues that they lose focus of what is really taking place. God is working deeply in their hearts and lives. They, however, are so focused on trying to speak in tongues that they fail to sense His powerful empowering presence.

The seeker should expect tongues, but he should focus his attention on God, and on what He is doing in his life. He should sense the presence of the Spirit inside. He should then yield his entire being, including his tongue, to God.

Fear of Receiving a False Experience

There is a final misunderstanding about receiving the Spirit that needs clearing up. Some people are afraid of seeking for the Spirit because they are afraid that they will receive a false or demonic experience. They have been ominously warned of the dangers of opening oneself up to the spirit world. They have been told that, once they open themselves up in such a way, an evil spirit can slip in and take control of their life. They have heard hair-raising stories about people who were possessed with evil spirits when they were seeking to be filled with the Spirit.

But such warnings are misleading, because Jesus promised that, if we ask of the Father, He will give to us only "good gifts" (Matt. 7:11). If you are truly seeking God, He will not allow you to receive a false spirit or a false experience. Jesus promised,

> For everyone who asks receives, and he who seeks finds, and to him who knocks it will be opened. If a son asks for bread from any father among you, will he give him a stone? Or if he

asks for a fish, will he give him a serpent instead of a fish? Or if he asks for an egg, will he offer him a scorpion? If you then, being evil, know how to give good gifts to your children, how much more will your heavenly Father give the Holy Spirit to those who ask him! (Luke 11:10-13)

Jesus' meaning is clear. If you ask God for the Holy Spirit, He will give you the Holy Spirit. He will not give you a false experience, nor will he allow the enemy to impose a false experience upon you. He will not give you a serpent, or a scorpion, or a stone. He will give you what you ask for—the precious Holy Spirit. Don't be afraid. Ask today, and God will give you this blessed Gift.

TO BE FILLED WITH THE SPIRIT, DO THIS

Are you a child of God? Do you desire the Spirit's infilling? You can receive the Holy Spirit right now. Just do this:

Approach the throne of grace boldly, knowing that Jesus has made the way clear (Heb. 10:19). Remember His promise, "Everyone who asks receives" (Luke 11:10). Don't doubt. The promise is yours (Acts 2:39).

Now *ask the Father for His gift* (Luke 11:9-13). Remember, He is more eager to give the gift than you are to receive. As you pray, be aware of the Spirit's coming at your request. You will sense His presence coming upon you and filling you.

It is now time to *receive the Spirit by faith.* Reach out and claim the promise as yours. Don't wait for the Spirit to force His way in. In faith, pray this simple prayer, "I am now full of the Holy Spirit" (cf. Mark 11:24). "Breathe" Him in (cf. John 20:22).

Sense His presence filling you.

Now, *begin to speak.* Speak out with joy and abandon, allowing the Holy Spirit to gush forth from deep inside—from your "innermost being" (John 7:37, NASB). Allow Him to use your vocal organs and lips to speak through you. When you begin speaking words in a language you have never learned, don't be afraid. God is filling you with His precious Holy Spirit. Yield yourself more and more to Him and let the words flow out of you. Do it with all of your heart, holding nothing back, trusting God to do his part.

Praise the Lord! You have been baptized in the Holy Spirit! You have tasted and you have discovered that the Lord is indeed very very good.

––––––––––––––––

The baptism in the Holy Spirit is the gateway into a life in step the Spirit. It should thus be the aim of every Christian to be filled with the Spirit. And it should be the goal of every pastor to see that everyone of his or her members has been baptized in the Holy Spirit.

We must not assume, however, that it is enough that one be initially filled with the Spirit and then do nothing else. A life in the Spirit must be nurtured and nourished. We will discuss this important issue in the next chapter.

CHAPTER 5

MAINTAINING
THE SPIRIT-FILLED LIFE

Things fall apart." That's a saying often heard Africa, where my wife, Sandy, and I have served as missionaries for the past sixteen years. And it's true. Anything in this life which is left to itself falls apart. It deteriorates. In physics this phenomenon is called entropy. In the material universe things move naturally from a state of order to disorder.

The same is true in our spiritual lives. Unless they are constantly maintained, they deteriorate. Paul instructed Timothy to maintain the touch of God that was on his life (2 Tim. 1:6). A life lived in step with the Spirit of God must be perpetually maintained.

A believer begins his or her spiritual life by being born of the Spirit. He should then be immediately baptized in the Spirit. As discussed earlier, this spiritual baptism opens the door to countless other spiritual blessings. The newly Spirit-baptized believer should not; however, make the mistake of presuming that, because He has been baptized in the Spirit, his spiritual journey has come to an end. It has, in fact, only begun. Neither should he make the mistake of thinking that, now that he has received the Spirit, he can relax and do nothing.

In this chapter we will discuss how the Spirit-baptized believer can maintain his or her walk in the Spirit. In doing so we will discuss two issues: the importance of maintaining the Spirit-filled life and guidelines for maintaining the Spirit-filled life.

THE IMPORTANCE OF MAINTAINING THE SPIRIT-FILLED LIFE

Must Be Constantly Renewed

The importance of the believer maintaining the Spirit-filled life cannot be overemphasized. Once a person has been baptized in the Holy Spirit, he would be very unwise to assume that there is nothing more for him to do to maintain his spiritual life. Bible commentator Don Stamps wrote,

> However powerful the initial coming of the Holy Spirit on the believer may be, if this does not find expression in a life of prayer, witness, and holiness, the experience will soon become a fading glory . . . The baptism in the Spirit brings the believer into a relationship with the Spirit that is to be renewed (Acts 4:31) and maintained (Eph. 5:18).[1]

Each Believer's Personal Responsibility

Every believer in Christ must accept personal responsibility to maintain his or her own spiritual life. Although pastors and

---

[1] Don Stamps, *The Full Life Study Bible; New International Version,* "Baptism in the Holy Spirit" (Springfield, MO: Life Publishers International, 1990), 1643.

Christian friends can encourage and inspire, the final responsibility lies with the individual Christian. Like King David, each believer must learn to encourage himself in the Lord (1 Sam. 30:6).

Failure to do this will eventually result in backsliding and a loss of power and relationship with the Lord. One could eventually even lose his or her salvation. Paul encouraged Timothy to "fan into flame the gift of God" that was in him (2 Tim. 1:6). Just as a campfire needs constant attention if it is to remain ablaze, our spiritual lives also need constant monitoring. When the camper goes to sleep, his fire goes out. When the Christian sleeps, his spiritual fire goes out. We must, therefore, maintain constant vigilance over our spiritual lives.

A fire needs occasional stirring if it is to remain white hot, and fuel must be continually added if it is to continue to flame brightly. In the same way, we must continually maintain our spiritual lives. This maintenance should include frequent spiritual checkups. Paul exhorted the Corinthians, "Examine yourselves to see whether you are in the faith" (2 Cor. 13:5). Each believer must accept personal responsibility for his or her own spiritual life. The one whose spiritual fire goes out has no one to blame but himself.

GUIDELINES FOR MAINTAINING
A SPIRIT-FILLED LIFE

One may ask, "If I am personally responsible to maintain my own spiritual life, what then must I do? What specific steps can I take to ensure that I continue to walk in the Spirit?" There are at least eight strategies one may employ in maintaining his Spirit-filled life, as follows:

Seek Fresh Refillings

First, if a Christian is to remain full of the Spirit, he or she must seek fresh infillings of the Spirit. As mentioned above, every believer in Christ should be baptized in the Holy Spirit soon after conversion (Acts 1:4-5; 8:14-17). This spiritual baptism is a wonderful life-changing experience. The believer must realize, however, that the baptism in the Holy Spirit it is not a once-and-forever cure-all experience. Every Spirit-filled believer should seek to be continually filled and refilled with the Spirit throughout his or her entire life.

On the Day of Pentecost the disciples were initially baptized in the Holy Spirit (Acts 2:4). They were later refilled with the Spirit (Acts 4:8, 31). Paul was first baptized in the Holy Spirit in the city of Damascus (Acts 9:17-18). He was again filled with the Spirit on the island of Cyprus (Acts 13:9). In Acts 19:6 the twelve Ephesian disciples were baptized in the Spirit when Paul laid hands on them. Later, he wrote the Ephesians, urging them to "be filled with the Spirit" (Eph. 5:18). Every believer needs to be baptized in the Spirit, but every believer also needs fresh refillings as he lives his Christian life.

A careful study of Paul's exhortation to the Ephesians to be filled with the Spirit (Eph. 5:18) reveals a powerful spiritual principle: we must each be repeatedly filled with the Spirit. The Greek verb translated "be filled" in this text is in the present passive imperative tense. This means that the phrase "be filled with the Spirit" could be accurately rendered "be *being* filled with the Spirit"[2] Stanley Horton wrote about this verse, "We are to keep being filled with the Spirit (5:18). This (as the Greek indicates) is not a one-time experience, but a continued filling or (better) repeated fillings, as the book of Acts suggests."[3] The Spirit-filled believer must know that, if he is to maintain the Spirit-filled walk, he should seek a fresh infilling of the Spirit each day of his life.

Jesus was speaking about receiving the Holy Spirit when he said, "Ask and it will be given to you; seek and you will find; knock and the door will be opened to you" (Luke 11:9, note v. 13). Horton points out that these three verbs (ask, seek, knock) all speak of continuous and repeated action:

> To emphasize this, Jesus said plainly, "Ask [keep asking], and it shall be given you; seek [keep on seeking], and ye shall find; knock [keep knocking], and it shall be opened unto you. For everyone that asketh [who keeps on asking, who is an 'asker'] receiveth [keeps on receiving]; and he that seeketh [who keeps on seeking, who is a seeker] findeth [keeps on finding]; and to

---

[2] Ralph W. Harris, *Complete Biblical Library*, "New Testament Study Bible, Galatians— Philemon," (Springfield, MO: World Library Press, 1989), 155.

[3] Stanley M. Horton, *What the Bible Says About the Holy Spirit* (Springfield, MO: Gospel Publishing House, 1976), 244.

him that knocketh [who makes it his practice to knock on doors] it shall be opened.[4]

To maintain the Spirit-filled life the Christian must continually seek new refillings with the Holy Spirit. He must continually ask, seek, and knock if he is to continue and progress in his life in the Spirit.

Pray Without Ceasing

Vigilant prayer is an essential discipline if a Christian is to maintain his or her walk in the Spirit. Paul wrote the Thessalonians telling them to "pray continually [or 'pray without ceasing,' KJV], . . . for this is God's will for you in Christ Jesus. Do not put out the Spirit's fire" (1 Thess. 5:17-19). Note carefully what Paul is saying here. He is saying that, if believers will pray continually, they will not make the mistake of extinguishing the Spirit's inner flame. We must, as Goodspeed translates the verse, "never give up praying."[5]

Paul instructed the Ephesian Christians in spiritual warfare (6:10-18). He ended his instructions by writing, "And pray in the Spirit on all occasions with all kinds of prayers and requests." In order to maintain our life in the Spirit, and be ready to do spiritual warfare, we should "pray in the Spirit on all occasions."

We should pray daily, asking the Spirit for His infilling and His guidance.

---

[4] Ibid.

[5] Edgar J. Goodspeed, *The New Testament: An American Translation* (Chicago: University of Chicago Press, 1948).

Our daily prayer should include prayer in tongues. Paul said, "He who speaks [prays] in a tongue edifies himself" (1 Cor. 14:4). That is why he said, "I would that everyone of you speak [pray] in tongues" (v. 5), and later, "I thank God that I speak [pray] in tongues more than all of you" (v. 18). Through prayer in tongues, we maintain a powerful spirit-to-Spirit communion with God.

Be Fervent in Worship

A third way that a Christian can keep in step wit the Spirit is through fervent worship. Worship holds an important place in the Spirit-filled life. It is through Spirit-anointed worship that are we are "raised . . . up with Christ and seated . . . with him in the heavenly realms" (Eph. 2:6). Such worship results in "times of refreshing . . . from the Lord" (Acts 3:19).

In order to remain in close fellowship with the Spirit we should seek out worship opportunities. These could include times private devotional worship. Great spiritual strength can come from these private worship times (Isa. 40:31). We should also worship with other Spirit-filled believers in church services. The Bible says, "Let us not give up meeting together, as some are in the habit of doing, but let us encourage one another—and all the more as you see the Day approaching" (Heb. 10:25).

When opportunities present themselves, we must enter into spiritual worship with our whole heart (Ps. 100:4). King David prayed, "Praise the Lord, O my soul; all my inmost being, bless his holy name" (Ps. 103:1).

Paul recommended to the Ephesian believers this powerful strategy for maintaining the Spirit-filled life. He first exhorted them to "be filled with the Spirit" (Eph. 5:18). Then, in the verses following, he told them how this may be done: "Speak to one another with psalms, hymns and spiritual songs. Sing and make music in your heart to the Lord, always giving thanks to God the Father for everything, in the name of the Lord Jesus Christ" (vv. 19-20). The teaching is clear. Worship is one powerful way of maintaining the Spirit-filled walk. As we worship in the Spirit, our own spirits are renewed; our faith is built up, our souls are refreshed, and we are empowered for spiritual battle.

Meditate on the Word

Daily meditation on the Word of God is another essential element for maintaining a Spirit-controlled life. Jesus said, "The Spirit gives life; the flesh counts for nothing. The words that I have spoken to you, are spirit and they are life" (John 6:63).

What Jesus said here about His own words, can also be said for all the words of Scripture—they are Spirit and they are life. As we read the Bible and meditate on its words, the Spirit of God speaks new life into our spirits. If we are to maintain our lives in the Spirit, we must dedicate ourselves to daily devotional reading of the Word of God. The Word of God is food for our spiritual man. It is through reading the word that our spirits receive new life and strength (Ps. 119:92-93).

It is not enough, however, to simply read the Bible and then do nothing about it. We must obey the Word and apply its truths to our lives. James wrote, "Do not merely listen to the word, and so deceive yourselves. Do what it says" (James 1:22). Jesus said that "everyone who hears these words of mine and does not put them into practice is like a foolish man who built his house on sand" (Matt. 7:26). When the trial comes, he will be unable to stand. Our spiritual lives are maintained, then, not be merely reading the Word of God, but by reading it and then doing what it says.

Walk by Faith

Another strategy we must employ, if we are to remain in step with the Spirit, is we must walk by faith. To walk by the Spirit is to walk by faith, and to walk by faith is to walk by the Spirit. The phrases are synonymous. Paul connects the walk of faith and the walk of the Spirit when he says, "For we through the Spirit, by faith, are waiting for the hope of righteousness" (Gal. 5:5, NASB). It is by faith that we receive the Holy Spirit (Gal. 3:2, 14), and it is by faith that we maintain our life in the Spirit (v. 3).

It is also through faith that spiritual gifts are released in the believer's life, resulting in miraculous works. Paul wrote, "Does God give you his Spirit and work miracles among you because you observe the law, or because you believe what you heard?" (v. 5). The obvious answer to Paul's rhetorical question is that we receive the Spirit and work miracles by faith.

In another place Paul wrote that God "has given us the Spirit as a deposit" in our lives. He continued, "Therefore . . . we live by faith, not by sight" (1 Cor. 5:5-7). The one who desires to live in the Spirit must, by faith, focus his attention on

the unseen things of the Spirit. He must walk by faith and not by sight.

Live a Yielded Life

A sixth thing one can do to maintain the Spirit's touch on his life is to learn to live a yielded life. Living a yielded life involves being submitted to the Spirit and His will. It also involves an attitude of openness to the Spirit's promptings. The one desiring to live a life in step with the Spirit must live in a state of constant readiness to obey the voice of the Holy Spirit.

Jesus lived such a yielded life. He testified concerning Himself, "I tell you the truth, the Son can do nothing by himself; he can do only what he sees his Father doing, because whatever the Father does the Son also does. For the Father loves the son and shows him all he does" (John 5:19-20). Jesus completely submitted Himself to the will of His Father. This even included His willingness to go to the cross (John 8:28-29).

In like manner, the apostles lived lives that were yielded to the Holy Spirit. Whatever they did, whether praying (Luke 24: 53; Acts 1:14; 3:1; 4:31), worshiping (Acts 11:15; 13:1-4), witnessing (Acts 1:8; 4:8, 31), ministering (Acts 6:8; 16:6-10), or even conducting church business meetings (Acts 15:28), they did all under the authority of the Holy Spirit. If we are to walk in constant communion with the Spirit, we too must learn to lives that are yielded to God and His purposes.

Cultivate a Sensitive Spirit

Another necessary requirement for living a Spirit-filled life is spiritual sensitivity. By this we mean the ability to sense in one's spirit what the Spirit is saying and doing. Such spiritual sensitivity is essential. The one who wants to truly follow the Spirit must be keen to listen to His voice. He must also be quick to respond to what the Spirit says—even to repent when necessary.

We tune our radios to the proper station in order to receive a clear signal. In like manner, we must learn to tune our spirits to the voice of the Spirit of God. The Bible says that we must not harden our hearts to the Spirit's voice (Heb. 3:8, 15; 4:7). One way of hardening our hearts to the Spirit's voice, and thus tuning out the Spirit, is to look with contempt on manifestations of the Spirit. Paul said, "Do not put out the Spirit's fire; do not treat prophecies with contempt" (1 Thess. 5:19-20). By treating prophecies with contempt we can put out the Spirit's fire in our hearts. We must never be guilty of this foolish sin against the Spirit.

Walk in Obedience

Obedient, holy living is another requirement for maintaining the Spirit-filled life. The Holy Spirit can be grieved, and our spiritual lives can be quenched by impure living. In Ephesians 4:29-31 Paul made a list of sins that grieve the Holy Spirit of God:

- Unwholesome talk (corrupt speech, foul words)
- Bitterness (grudges and resentful thoughts)
- Rage (uncontrolled anger)
- Anger (desire to hurt and fight back)
- Brawling (railing, clamor)
- Slander (abusive and insulting language)
- Malice (desire to hurt for revenge)

Such unholy actions and attitudes will quench the Spirit's moving in our lives. They will grieve Him and cause Him to depart.

On the other hand, as we obey the voice of the Spirit, His presence grows stronger. At the same time, we learn to better follow Him (Heb. 5:14). As The Spirit prompts us to witness, to manifest spiritual gifts, and to pray, we must be quick to obey. As we do, we grow stronger in our spiritual lives.

Life is the Spirit is not an automatic thing. It must be maintained. We maintain our spiritual lives by giving diligent attention to them and to the things of the Spirit. We must never be guilty of allowing the flame of God's Spirit to go out in our lives.

- CHAPTER 6 -

THE FELLOWSHIP
OF THE HOLY SPIRIT

We can know God, the Father; we can know Jesus, the Son; but, someone may ask, can we *really* know the Holy Spirit? The answer to that question is a resounding "Yes!" And we can know Him intimately.

The apostle Paul concluded his second letter to the Corinthians with a blessing: "May the grace of the Lord Jesus Christ, and the love of God, and the fellowship of the Holy Spirit be with you all" (2 Cor. 13:14). Notice the phrase "fellowship of the Holy Spirit." This fellowship of the Spirit is a wonderful privilege of every Spirit-filled Christian.

In our last chapter we talked about how a Christian can maintain his or her walk in the Spirit. In this chapter we will discuss how a believer may live in daily fellowship with the Spirit of God. In our discussion of this topic we will ask and answer three questions: (1) What is meant by the term "fellowship of the Holy Spirit"? (2) Why do we each need this wonderful fellowship with the Spirit? and (3) How can one live

in daily fellowship with the Spirit of God? Let's begin by

addressing the first question.

WHAT IS MEANT BY THE FELLOWSHIP OF THE SPIRIT?

What the Fellowship of the Spirit is Not

Before we discuss what is meant by the term "fellowship with the Holy Spirit," let's first talk about what it does *not* mean. It does not mean the following:

1. Simply "having the Spirit." Fellowship with the Holy Spirit does not mean that one has simply been born again, or even filled with the Spirit. It is more than merely "having the Spirit." Although it involves both being born of the Spirit and being filled with the Spirit (as we will discuss later) it does not stop there.

2. A one-time event. Fellowship with the Spirit is not a single event in the Christian life. Nor is it even a series of events. It is, rather, a daily walk with the Spirit of God. It may involve events and experiences with the Holy Spirit, but it is much more.

What the Fellowship of the Spirit Is

If fellowship of the Spirit is more than an experience or an event in the Christian life, then, what exactly is it? Fellowship with the Holy Spirit is a life of intimate, daily communion with God through the Holy Spirit.

In order for us to fully understand the concept of the fellowship of the Holy Spirit, it is important that we first know the biblical meaning of the word fellowship. The Greek word which in 2 Corinthians 13:14 is translated "fellowship," (or

76

"communion" in some translations) is *koinonia*. This word means much more than casual acquaintance. It speaks of more than spending social time together, as at a church social or fellowship meeting. The word *koinonia* means deep, loving communion. It means the sharing of common experiences. It is the intimate communion that takes place within a family and between a husband and his wife.

This fellowship with the Holy Spirit is a precious thing. It brings us into a loving relationship with each member of the blessed Godhead—the Father, the Son, and the Holy Spirit. Let's look briefly at each of these relationships.

1. Fellowship with the Father. The fellowship of the Holy Spirit brings us into close communion with our Heavenly Father. The Bible teaches that it is through the Holy Spirit that God pours out His love into our hearts (Rom. 5:5). As the Holy Spirit moves in a believer's spirit, the believer is able to more fully comprehend God's love, and he is inspired to respond to that love (1 John 4:19). As a result of this deep love he feels for God, he is inspired to cry out, "Abba, Father!" (Rom. 8:15). In this way the Holy Spirit will bring us into an intimate relationship with our Heavenly Father.

2. Fellowship with the Son. The Holy Spirit will also bring us into intimate relationship with the Son. The night before Jesus was crucified, He said to His disciples, "I will not leave you as orphans; I will come to you" (John 14:18). He was speaking of coming to them in the person of the Holy Spirit. On the same occasion, He also told them that the Father would send the Holy Spirit in His name (v. 26). And later that same night, Jesus told His disciples more of what the work of the Holy Spirit would be:

But when he, the Spirit of truth, comes, he will guide you into all truth. He will not speak on his own; he will speak only what he hears, and he will tell you what is yet to come. He will bring glory to me by taking from what is mine and making it known to you. (John 16:13-14)

According to this passage, the Holy Spirit brings us into fellowship with Jesus in three ways: First, He guides us into all truth. (Jesus had just told his disciples the He was the truth, [14:6].) Next, He brings glory to Jesus. And, finally, He takes what belongs to Jesus and gives it to us. As the believer walks in fellowship with the Spirit, he is consequently brought into a more intimate relationship with Jesus.

3. Fellowship with the Holy Spirit. Not only will the Holy Spirit bring us into an intimate relationship with the Father and the Son, He will also bring us into a loving relationship with Himself. When the Bible speaks of the fellowship of the Holy Spirit, it is certainly referring to the sweet communion each believer can have with the Spirit Himself. In the remainder of this chapter we will focus our attention on this wonderful relationship we can have with the Spirit of God.

WHY WE NEED THE FELLOWSHIP OF THE SPIRIT

We must all learn to walk in close fellowship with the Holy Spirit for at least two reasons:

We Need His Loving Companionship

The first reason we need to live in close communion with the Holy Spirit is that we need His loving companionship. Before Jesus went back to heaven He promised, "I will come unto you" (John 14:18). He comes to us today in the person of the Holy Spirit. Jesus called the Holy Spirit "another Counselor" (v. 16). The Greek words which are here translated "another Counselor," *allos parakletos,* make an interesting word study. The noun *parakletos* literally means "one who comes along side to help." The adjective, *allos,* means another of the same sort.

By calling the Holy Spirit *"allos parakletos"* Jesus was saying that the Spirit would come to take His place. In other words, the Holy Spirit would come to us and abide with us, just as Jesus would if He were here in the flesh. What wonderful, loving companionship His presence provides to us. How we need this presence of God in our lives. Like Moses, we must pray, "If your Presence does not go with us, do not send us from here" (Exod. 33:15).

How the disciples must have despaired when Jesus told them that He was going away. And how they must have doubted when He said, "It is to your advantage that I go away" (John 16:7, NASB). How could such a thing have been to their advantage? It is almost unthinkable, and yet, it was true.

79

The advantage was that He would return to them in the person of the Holy Spirit. Then, He would not only be *with* them, He would be *in* them (John 14:17). Much more, not only would He be with *them*, but He would be with *every* born again believer at all times, in every place, in the entire world. Imagine how much it would help if Jesus was with you everywhere you went. And it is true, He does go with you, if you are indwelt by the Holy Spirit.

We Need His Strong Assistance

Another reason we need the fellowship of the Holy Spirit is that we need the Spirit's strong assistance in our lives. Consider this: the word *parakletos* does not simply mean one who comes along side, it means one who comes along side to lend assistance. The Holy Spirit will come to us and help us in every area of our service for God. Later in this book, we will discuss in detail many of the benefits of the Spirit's indwelling presence. Here, we will briefly mention only three:

1. In witnessing. Jesus promised that the Holy Spirit would enable believers to witness. He enables them in at least two ways: The first is by *empowering them to witness* (Acts 1:8). With this divine empowering comes anointing for ministry (Luke 4:18-19; Acts 10:38), which includes the manifestation of spiritual gifts (1 Cor. 12:8-11). Another way He enables believers is by *imparting the nature of Christ* into their lives. This nature is exemplified by the nine fruit of the Spirit listed in Galatians 5:22-23.

2. In preaching and teaching. Not only will the Holy Spirit enable believers to witness for Christ, He will also enable them in other kinds of ministry. He will aid the Christian worker in his or her preaching and teaching. Just as the Spirit anointed the preaching and teaching ministry of Jesus and the apostles, He will also anoint our ministries today. With this anointing will come greater understanding and greater persuasive power. The anointing will also provide divine insight into the Scriptures and into the needs of the people. As a result, our preaching and teaching ministries will be greatly enhanced.

3. In conflict with evil. A third way a relationship with the Spirit will assist us in our ministries is by giving us power over evil spirits (Matt. 12:28; Luke 10:19). Gospel ministry involves challenging and defeating demons (Mark 16:17). Demonic powers can only be defeated in the power of God. Here again, the Spirit will be with us to help us defeat Satan. The Holy Spirit dwells in us, and He is the One who is stronger than the demonic strong man (1 John 4:4; Matt. 12:29). How we need the power and anointing of the Spirit in our ministries.

There are more ways that the Spirit will come along side us to help us in our service for God; however, these three should serve as encouraging examples. We will discuss these topics in more detail in the last three chapters of this book.[1]

---

[1] You can learn more about the Spirit's power to overcome Satan by reading the author's book *Power Ministry: How to Minister in the Spirit's Power,* published by Africa's Hope, Springfield, MO, USA.

HOW WE CAN LIVE IN DAILY FELLOWSHIP WITH THE SPIRIT

We have discussed how the fellowship of the Holy Spirit can help us in our lives and in our ministries. We will now answer the question, "What must one do if he or she is to live in daily fellowship with the Holy Spirit?" In answering this question we will address three pertinent issues: (1) the prerequisites for living in daily fellowship with the Spirit, (2) the problem we must overcome if we are to live in daily fellowship

with the Spirit, and (3) the plan that we must follow if we are to live in daily fellowship with the Spirit.

The Prerequisites

It makes sense that, before one can continue in fellowship with the Spirit, he must first begin his life in the Spirit. There are, therefore, two essential spiritual experiences that one needs to live in true and intimate fellowship with the Holy Spirit: he must have been born again by the Spirit of God, and he must have been baptized in the Holy Spirit. These two fundamental spiritual experiences are prerequisites for a life of intimate fellowship with the Spirit. Let's look briefly at each:

1. Born of the Spirit (John 3:1-7). Before one can live in fellowship with the Spirit he or she must first be born of the Spirit. We begin our Christian lives with the Spirit of God (Gal. 3:3). Jesus referred to this new beginning as being born again (John 3:3-7). He said that "flesh gives birth to flesh, but the Spirit gives birth to spirit" (v. 6).

82

Only the Holy Spirit can impart spiritual life to an individual. Before one is born again, that person has no capacity to commune with God. The Bible says that the man without the Spirit cannot understand spiritual things (1 Cor. 2:14). However, as a result of this new Spirit-given life, a person can now perceive spiritual things. He can "see the kingdom of God" (John 3:3). Before one can live in fellowship with the Spirit, he or she must be truly born from above.

   2. *Filled with the Spirit (Acts 2:1-4).* If a person is to live in daily fellowship with the Spirit, not only must he be born of the Spirit, he must also be filled with the Spirit. Jesus characterized this infilling with the Spirit as a baptism in the Holy Spirit (Acts 1:5). This baptism in the Spirit enlarges one's capacity for spiritual things. The Holy Spirit, who enters one's life at the new birth, is now given greater access into every area of his or her life. Once a believer has been filled with the Spirit, he is more acutely aware of the Spirit's indwelling presence, and his life is more fully energized by the Spirit's abiding power.

   The disciples of Jesus are the best illustration of this fact. Before they were baptized in the Holy Spirit on the Day of Pentecost, they had very little spiritual understanding and power. After they were filled with the Holy Spirit, things were dramatically different. They demonstrated a spiritual power and sensitivity to the Spirit they did not have before (Acts 11:12; 13:1-4; 15:28). The same is true today. The infilling with the Holy Spirit is an absolute necessity for any person who wants to live in close communion with the Spirit of God.

The Problem

And yet there is a problem with many whose lives have been touched by the Spirit of God. Many believers, once they have been born again, stop there. They never progress any further in their spiritual experience. They think that through this one experience they have received all there is to receive from God. They do not understand that they must now go on to be filled with the Spirit (Eph. 5:18).

There is, however, a similar problem among Pentecostal believers. Many, once they are baptized in the Holy Spirit, stop there, and go no further in their spiritual experience. They foolishly view the experience of Spirit baptism as a finish line in the Christian experience, when in reality, it is only the starting line. As we described it in Chapter 3, the baptism in the Holy Spirit is simply the gateway into the Spirit-filled life. It is not to be viewed simply a goal to be achieved, or a spiritual trophy to be attained. It is rather a glorious entrance into greater service and fellowship with God.

The Plan

Once a person has been born again and filled with the Spirit, he must now aim to live in daily fellowship with the Spirit. But what must he do to achieve this blessed fellowship? He must have a plan for advancement in his spiritual life.

Building a relationship with the Spirit of God is much like building a relationship with any other person. If one wants to build a stronger relationship with someone else, he must plan to spend time with that person. How else could he get to know that individual? In like manner, if we are going to grow in our relationship with the Holy Spirit, we must spend time communing with the Holy Spirit. There are two dynamic ways that we can commune with the Spirit:

1. Prayer in the Spirit. The first way we can spend time in communion with the Holy Spirit is by praying in the Spirit. As we pray in the Spirit, we grow in our relationship with the Him. By prayer in the Spirit we mean prayer in tongues (1 Cor. 14:2). As we thus pray in the Spirit, our relationship with the Holy Spirit grows and becomes stronger. Paul (now David) Yonggi Cho, pastor of the largest church in the world, Yoido Full Gospel Church in Seoul, Korea, gives this testimony:

> I also speak tongues very much. Speaking in tongues is the Holy Spirit's language, and when I speak in tongues, I cannot help but experience His presence in my consciousness. In my own personal prayer life I pray in tongues more than 60 percent of the time. I pray in tongues when I sleep. I wake up praying in tongues. I pray in tongues while I am studying the Bible, and I pray in tongues during my personal devotions. If somehow I ever lost the gift of the tongues, I think my ministry would be whittled down to about 50 percent of what it is now. Whenever I speak in tongues, I cannot help but keep the Holy Spirit in my consciousness.[2]

Paul said, "If I pray in a tongue, my spirit prays" (1 Cor. 14:14). As the Spirit of God moves on and in the Spirit-filled believer, the believer's spirit begins to pray. At such a time an intimate communion takes place between the believer and the Holy Spirit. Could this have been why Paul said, "I thank God that I speak in tongues more than all of you"? (v. 18).

2. Prayer to the Spirit. The one desiring a more intimate

---

[2] Paul Cho Yonggi, *Successful Home Cell Groups* (Alachua, FL: Bridge Logos Publishers, 1981), 131.

relationship with the Holy Spirit should not only pray *in* the Spirit, he should also pray *to* the Spirit. This is a second way we can spend time in communion with the Holy Spirit.

Just as the Father and Jesus are Persons to whom we can talk, the blessed Holy Spirit is also a Person to whom we can talk and commune. Cho further commented on this kind of prayer:

> Also, I always try to spend at least one hour with the Holy Spirit the first thing every morning. No matter what happens, I want to give Him that one hour. "Dear Holy Spirit," I will say, "let's have a session together. Let's read the Bible together." And so together the Holy Spirit and I sit down and praise God. I worship Jesus and I read the Scriptures. I love the Holy Spirit, and I praise Him, and together we plan the work.[3]

When may we spend time in communion with the Spirit? Like pastor Cho, we can spend time with Him in the early morning hours before we begin our day's work. We can commune with him all through the day. As we go about our daily activities, we can pray quietly in the Spirit. We can also fellowship with him as we lay on our beds at night, just before we drop off to sleep. In fact, we can commune with the Holy Spirit any time, day or night. He is the Remarkable Friend who

is always with us to bless and help us. We must learn to know Him better and better each day.

---

[3]Ibid, 130.

What a wonderful privilege we have, this privilege of fellowship with the Spirit of God. How foolish we will be if we neglect this wonderful opportunity. We should all make it our goal to live in constant, daily fellowship with the Holy Spirit.

CHAPTER 7

WALKING

IN THE SPIRIT

L egend has it that in the rainforests of the Democratic Republic of Congo there is a tribal group whose custom is to never allow their king's feet to touch the ground. When he wants to move from place to place, he is carried in a royal litter by specially-appointed servants. When he alights from his litter, a mat is always placed on the ground so that his feet will not touch the soil.

Things are much different for the common people of Malawi, where My wife, Sandy, and I lived and ministered for fifteen years. Walking makes up a large part of their daily lives. Well over 90% of Malawians don't own cars, and most don't even own a bicycle. As a result, Malawians spend many hours each week walking from place to place. So, when they read Paul's injunction to "walk in the Spirit," they naturally associate it with the very fabric of their lives.

Writing to the churches of Galatia, Paul encouraged the Christians to live their lives under the control of the Holy Spirit. "Since we live by the Spirit" he said, "let us keep in step with the Spirit" (Gal. 5:25). Not only were they to begin their Christian lives in the Spirit, they were to continue to live under the Spirit's control.

In this chapter we will focus much of our attention on the books of Galatians and Romans, where Paul deals comprehensively with this subject. I recommend that you keep your Bible opened to these books as you work your way through this chapter. We will discuss three aspects of walking in the Spirit: (1) the importance of walking in the Spirit, (2) what it means to walk in the Spirit, and (3) how to walk in the Spirit. Let's begin by examining the importance of walking in the Spirit.

THE IMPORTANCE OF WALKING IN THE SPIRIT

Too often we Pentecostals emphasize being filled in the Holy Spirit, but neglect teaching on the subject of walking in the Spirit. This is indeed tragic, and has caused the spiritual lives of many Christians to be stunted. If we are to grow in Christ, and live effective Christian lives, we must learn how to walk in the Spirit.

Paul Appeals to Our Sense of Reason

Notice how in Galatians 5:25 the apostle appealed to the Galatian believers' sense of reason. His argument was as follows: Since you have begun your new life in Christ through the enablement of the Holy Spirit, doesn't it now make sense that you should continue your life in Him in the same way? Note the two parts of his argument:

1. We live by the Spirit. Paul begins his argument by reminding the Galatian believers about how they began their

Christian walk—they began it in the Spirit. There is, in fact, no other way to begin the Christian life. Jesus was very straightforward in His teaching on the subject:

> I tell you the truth, no one can see the kingdom of God unless he is born again . . . no one can enter the kingdom of God unless he is born of water and the Spirit. Flesh gives birth to flesh, but the Spirit gives birth to spirit. You should not be surprised at my saying, "You must be born again." (John 3:3, 5-7)

We begin our Christian life through the regenerative work of the Spirit. In the above passage Jesus says three things about how the Spirit introduces us to our new life in Christ:

- First, the Spirit opens our eyes to the things of God: "No one can see the kingdom of God unless he is born again" (v. 3).
- Next, the Spirit gives us entrance into the kingdom of God: "No one can enter the kingdom of God unless he is born of . . . the Spirit" (v. 5).
- Finally, the Spirit regenerates us and gives a new birth: "Spirit gives birth to spirit . . . So it is with everyone born of the Spirit" (vv. 6, 8).

As we have already emphasized in previous chapters, in addition to beginning the Christian life by being born of the Spirit, every believer should also begin his Christian life by being immediately baptized in the Holy Spirit. In Galatians 5:25 Paul was reminding the Galatians *both* of their new birth *and* their Spirit baptism. We believe this to be true since Paul had just discussed the subject of Spirit baptism with them:

> I would like to learn just one thing from you: Did you receive the Spirit by observing the law, or by believing what you heard? . . . Does God give you his Spirit and work miracles among you because you observe the law, or because you believe what you heard? . . . He redeemed us in order that the blessing given to Abraham might come to the Gentiles through Christ, so that by faith we might receive the promise of the Spirit. (Gal. 3:2, 14)

These Galatian believers (according to the New Testament pattern of Acts 2:38-39) had been filled with the Spirit soon after being born again (13:52). They were now alive by the Spirit of God. They had begun their spiritual lives by being born again and being baptized in the Holy Spirit. Believers today should begin the same way. They should first be born of the Spirit; then they should immediately be filled with the Spirit.

2. We must walk by the Spirit. Paul is reasoning like this: since the Galatians began their new lives in Christ through the powerful inner working of the Holy Spirit, they should now let the Spirit continue His work in them, directing their lives. The New English Bible translates Galatians 5:25 this way: "If the Spirit is the source of our life, let the Spirit also direct its course."

Paul is, in effect, saying, "Now that you have the Spirit, you should let the Spirit have you!" He exhorts the Galatian believers, "Are you so foolish? After beginning with the Spirit, are you now trying to attain your goal by human effort?" (3:3).

The following chart helps to illustrate the differences between living by the Spirit and walking by the Spirit:

Living by the Spirit and Walking by the Spirit	
Living by the Spirit	**Walking by the Spirit**
We begin our new walk in Christ.	We continue our new walk in Christ.
Through the new birth, the Spirit gives us new life	Under the Spirit's direction, we now walk in newness of life; that is, we walk as Christ walked.
Through the infilling of the Spirit we are given power to be a witnesses.	We now walk in the power and anointing of the Spirit. We use the Spirit's power to witness and do the works of Jesus.

Jesus, Our Great Example

Jesus is our great example of One who lived and walked in the Spirit. He is the living illustration of the concepts we are discussing in this book. There are many ways Jesus serves as an example of how we should walk in the Spirit. We will mention three:

1. He was filled with the Spirit. When Jesus was baptized by John in the Jordan River, He actually received two baptisms. He was both baptized in water and baptized in the Holy Spirit. The Bible says, "When all the people were being baptized, Jesus was baptized too. And as he was praying, heaven was opened and the Holy Spirit descended on him in bodily form like a dove . . ." (Luke 3:21-22). From that moment on, Jesus was filled with, and anointed by, the Holy Spirit (Luke 4:1, 14, 18-19; John 1:32-33; Acts 10:38). Before He returned to heaven, Jesus commanded His followers to be filled with the Holy Spirit, just as He was (Luke 24:49; Acts 1:4-5).

2. *He received direction from the Spirit.* Jesus testified that everything He did, He did under the guidance of His heavenly Father (John 5:19-20, 8:28, 12:49). This divine guidance came to Him through the Holy Spirit (Matt. 4:1; Mark 1:12; Luke 4:1). Just as Jesus received guidance and direction from the Father by the Spirit, we as His followers, should in the same way receive direction from God through the Holy Spirit.

3. *He ministered by the Spirit's power.* Although Jesus was the eternal Son of God, He chose not to minister in His own divine power (Phil. 2:7). He rather chose to minister only in the power of the Holy Spirit (Luke 4:18-19; Acts 10:38). This is most clearly seen in the gospel of Luke:

- "When all the people were being baptized, Jesus was baptized too. And as he was praying, heaven was opened and the Holy Spirit descended on him in bodily form like a dove . . ." (3:21-22).
- "Jesus, full of the Holy Spirit, returned from Jordan and was led by the Spirit in the desert . . ." (4:1-2).
- "Jesus returned to Galilee in the power of the Spirit..." (4:14).
- Jesus testified, "The Spirit of the Lord is upon me, because he has anointed me . . ." (4:18).
- "One day as he was teaching . . . the power of the Lord was present for him to heal the sick" (5:17).
- "And the people all tried to touch him, because power

was coming from him and healing them all" (6:19).

We must ask the question, "Why, if Jesus was Himself God, did He choose to minister in the power of the Holy Spirit rather than in His own power?" The answer is clear. He wanted to be an example to us. He wanted to show us how we, too, can minister in the same power and with the same results (cf. John 14:12-16).

WHAT IT MEANS TO WALK IN THE SPIRIT

We have discussed the importance of every Christian walking in the Spirit. We will now discuss what it means to walk in the Spirit. A close examination of Paul's teaching on the subject in the books of Galatians and Romans reveals that walking by the Spirit means at least four things:

To Walk in Holiness

First, to walk by the Spirit means to walk in holiness of heart and life. Paul instructed the Galatians believers, "Live by the Spirit, and you will not gratify the desires of the sinful nature" (5:16). He further said that those who "belong to Christ Jesus" must learn to walk in the Spirit by "crucif[ying] the sinful

nature" (v. 24). As we thus follow the dictates of the Holy Spirit, we will be lead into a life of Christ-like holiness.

In Romans Paul called the Holy Spirit "the Spirit of holiness" (1:4) Later in the same letter, he said that, through the power of the Spirit, "the righteous requirements of the law might be fully met in us" (8:4). Thus, as one lives his or her life under the rule of the Holy Spirit, there will be two results:

95

1. Compelled to live holy. The Spirit-filled believer will be compelled to live a holy life. The Holy Spirit will be present in his life creating in him a greater awareness of the holiness of God. The Spirit will also produce in him a heightened sensitivity to sin, convicting him whenever he is tempted to go astray (John 16:8-11).

2. Empowered to live holy. Not only will the Spirit compel the Spirit-filled believer to live a holy life, He will also empower him to do the same. The Spirit will be present in him to give him power to triumph over temptation and sin (Rom. 8:1-4, 13). The Spirit-filled Christian will thus be enabled to live a victorious, Christ-like life (Gal. 5:22-23).

To Walk in Love

Not only does walking by the Spirit mean to walk in holiness of life, it also means to walk in love. In Galatians 5, immediately before Paul talked about walking in the Spirit (v. 25), he talked about the fruit of the Spirit (vv. 22-24). He began by saying "the fruit of the Spirit is love . . ."

The Bible teaches that it is through the Holy Spirit that we experience God's love: "God has poured out his love into our hearts by the Holy Spirit, whom he has given us" (Rom. 5:5). Further, it is by the Holy Spirit that we are kept in His love: "But you, dear friends, build yourselves up in your most holy faith and pray in the Holy Spirit. Keep yourselves in God's love . . ." (Jude 20-21). No one can say that he is truly walking in the Spirit if he does not demonstrate the love of God in his attitudes and actions.

To Walk in Submission to the Spirit

Further, to walk by the Spirit means to walk in submission

to the Holy Spirit. Paul taught that "those who live in accordance with the Spirit have their minds set on what the Spirit desires" (Rom. 8:5). The person who is walking in the Spirit has submitted his or her own will to the will of the Holy Spirit. He is no longer motivated by his own selfish desires, but he humbly and cheerfully submits himself to the desires of the Spirit. Paul said, "We should let the Spirit direct the course of our lives" (Gal 5:25, NEB).

Self-will is the enemy of the Spirit-filled life. Until we are willing to fully submit our wills to the will of God, we will never fully walk by the Spirit. We have but two choices: We can either "gratify the desires of the sinful nature," thus living a life "contrary to the Spirit" (Gal 5:17), or we can submit ourselves to the desires of the Spirit and live a life "in step with the Spirit" (Gal 5:25).

To Walk in Faith

Finally, to walk by the Spirit also means to walk in faith. A life in the Spirit is, in fact, a life of faith. Jesus said that the living waters of the Spirit would flow out of "whoever believes" (John 7:38). Paul asked the Galatians, "I would like to learn just one thing from you: Did you receive the Spirit by observing the law, or by believing what you heard? Are you so foolish? After beginning with the Spirit are you now trying to attain your goal by human effort?" (Gal. 3:2-3).

The Galatian believers had begun their life in the Spirit by "believing what [they] heard." By faith, they had received the promise of the Spirit (v. 14). In addition, God had given them His Spirit and worked miracles among them because they had believed what they had heard (v. 5). Their life in the Spirit was, from first to last, a life of faith. The same is true today. The person who would walk in the Spirit, must learn to walk in faith.

REQUIREMENTS FOR WALKING IN THE SPIRIT

We have discussed the importance of walking in the Spirit and what it means to walk in the Spirit. We will now turn our attention to three essential requirements for walking in the Spirit:

Be Born of the Spirit

As we have indicated above, the first essential requirement for walking in the Spirit is being born of the Spirit. No one should ever be so foolish as to think that he or she can walk in the Spirit without ever being born of the Spirit.

Have you been born from above? (John 3:3-7). Have you become a new creation in Christ? (2 Cor. 5:17). You can receive

new life in Christ today by repenting of your sins and by putting your faith in Jesus Christ as Lord and Savior.

Be Filled and Refilled with the Spirit

In addition to being born of the Spirit, the one who desires to walk in the Spirit must be continually filled with the Spirit. We have already mentioned this fact at the beginning of this chapter, but we feel that this point needs more discussion now.

We must never forget that being filled with the Spirit involves two things: It involves being initially baptized in the Holy Spirit, and it involves repeated refillings with the Spirit.

We see this truth demonstrated in Paul's dealings with the Ephesian church. When, during his third missionary journey, Paul first arrived in the city of Ephesus, he met twelve disciples. He immediately asked them, "Did you receive the Holy Spirit when you believed?" (Acts 19:2). Discovering that they had never been baptized in the Spirit, he "placed his hands on them, the Holy Spirit came on them, and they spoke in tongues and prophesied" (v. 6). They were, at that moment, initially baptized in the Holy Spirit.

However, sometime later, Paul wrote these same Ephesian Christians, encouraging them to continue in the Spirit: "Do not get drunk on wine. . ." he exhorted, "but be filled with the Spirit" (Eph. 5:18). It was not sufficient for them to have been baptized in the Spirit some months or years in the past; they must be presently empowered by the Holy Spirit.

In a similar manner, Paul exhorted Timothy, his younger colleague and the missionary-pastor of the church in Ephesus, to "stir up the gift of God" which was in him by the laying on of Paul's hands (2 Tim. 1:6). He was telling the Ephesians, pastor and people alike, that they should seek fresh refillings of the Holy Spirit. They should learn to daily walk in the Spirit's power and fellowship.

One may ask, "How can one receive such daily infillings of the Holy Spirit?" Jesus answers this question for us: "Ask and it will be given to you; seek and you will find; knock and the door will be opened to you" (Luke 11:9). We know that Jesus was here talking about receiving the Holy Spirit for He immediately said, "If you then, though you are evil, know how to give good gifts to your children, how much more will your Father in heaven give the Holy Spirit to those who ask him!" (v. 13).

The tense of the Greek verbs in this verse indicate repeated or continuous action. A more literal translation of verse 9, as discussed in Chapter 5, would therefore be, "Keep on asking and you will keep on receiving; keep on seeking and you will keep on finding; keep on knocking and doors will continually be opened unto you." The secret to continued refillings of the Holy Spirit is continued asking. We should daily—even several times each day—ask the Holy Spirit to fill us.

This truth is also taught in Ephesians 5:18, where Paul said, "Be filled with the Spirit." Don Stamps comments on this verse:

> "Be filled" (present passive imperative) carries the meaning in the Greek of "repeatedly being filled." God's children must experience constant renewal (3:14-19; 4:22-24; Rom. 12:2) by repeatedly being filled with the Holy Spirit . . . Christians are to be baptized in the Holy Spirit after conversion (see Acts 1:5;

> 2:4), yet they are to filled with the Spirit repeatedly for worship, service and witness . . .[1]

We conclude: To walk in the Spirit one must be continually filled with the Spirit. This continual filling with the Spirit involves both being initially baptized in the Spirit and daily repeated refillings with the Holy Spirit.

Sow to the Spirit

---

[1] Don Stamps, *Full Life Study Bible: New International Version* (Springfield, MO: Life Publishers International, 1990), 1834.

A third essential requirement for walking by the Spirit is "sowing to the Spirit." Paul further taught that we walk in the Spirit by sowing to the Spirit: "The one who sows to please his sinful nature, from that nature will reap destruction; the one who sows to please the Spirit; from the Spirit will reap eternal life" (Gal. 6:8).

It is important that we understand the literary context of this verse—a discussion on living by the Spirit (5:16, 25). In Galatians 5:16-6:9 Paul contrasted sowing to the Spirit with sowing to the sinful nature. He taught that sowing to the sinful nature produces a harvest of fleshy acts (5:19-20), and eventually results in destruction (6:8). Just the opposite happens when one sows to the Spirit. Sowing to the Spirit results in a harvest of spiritual fruit (5:22-23) and results in eternal life (6:8).

One way we can sow to the Spirit is by focusing our thoughts on the things of the Spirit of God. Paul taught that "those who live in accordance with the Spirit have their minds set on what the Spirit desires" (Rom. 8:5-9). We must never allow the things of the world to distract us from the things that God desires.

Another way a Christian can sow to the Spirit is to do those things that please the Spirit of God. These things include holy living, acts of love and kindness, and quick obedience to the Word of God. It should be the aim of every Christian to live his life under the Spirit's control. "If we live by the Spirit, we should also walk by the Spirit."

CHAPTER 8

SPEAKING IN TONGUES
WHAT GOOD IS IT?

My friend and I had been talking for over an hour. The young Baptist preacher had come to my home to discuss being filled with the Holy Spirit. As we talked about the benefits of the Spirit-filled life, he became more and more excited. Then, I said to him, "When you are filled with the Spirit you will speak in tongues." I watched as his face fell. He asked apprehensively, "Do I *have* to speak in tongues?" I replied, "No, you don't *have* to speak in tongues, you *get* to speak in tongues. It is not a punishment. It is the wonderful privilege of every Spirit-filled believer!" Then he asked me, "But what good is speaking in tongues?"

In this chapter we will seek to answer my friend's query about speaking in tongues. In doing this, we will answer two important questions: (1) what is speaking in tongues? and (2) what good is it?

WHAT IS SPEAKING IN TONGUES?

It is important that we have a very clear idea of what speaking in tongues actually is. We need this understanding in our own spiritual walk. We also need to understand the practice of speaking in tongues so we can explain its meaning and uses to others.

Often Spoken About in the New Testament

As with the baptism in the Holy Spirit, the practice of speaking in tongues is not an invention of the modern Pentecostal or charismatic movements. Speaking in tongues was the common practice of New Testament Christians. Tongues are often spoken about in the New Testament. Let's look at five places where the practice of speaking in tongues is mentioned:

1. The Great Commission. In His Great Commission to the church Jesus told His disciples that they would speak in new tongues. He said that speaking in tongues was to be one of the signs of believers as they went into all the world to preach the gospel: "And these signs will accompany those who believe: In my name they will drive out demons; they will speak in new tongues" (Mark 16:17).

The implication is obvious. As we go forth preaching the gospel, we should expect the new believers to speak in tongues. This ability to speak in tongues comes from being baptized in the Holy Spirit (Acts 2:4). The message of the baptism in the Spirit is a central feature of true gospel preaching (Acts 2:17-18, 33, 38-39; 3:19-20).

2. The Day of Pentecost. When the Holy Spirit was poured out on the Day of Pentecost "all of them were filled with the

Holy Spirit and began to speak in other tongues as the Spirit enabled them" (Acts 2:4). Not only did the twelve apostles speak in tongues, but every one of the 120 believers who were gathered with them spoke in tongues. This group included Mary, the mother of Jesus, as well as the brothers of Jesus (Acts 1:14).

3. The Book of Acts. Throughout the book of Acts we discover believers speaking in tongues. The first time was on the Day of Pentecost, as mentioned above. Another is found in Acts 10. On this occasion the Holy Spirit came upon the people gathered at the house of Cornelius. As a result, "they heard them speaking in tongues and praising God" (v. 46). More than twenty years later, when Paul, on his third missionary journey, arrived in Ephesus, he found twelve disciples. The Bible says, "When Paul placed his hands on them, the Holy Spirit came on them, and they spoke in tongues and prophesied" (Acts 19:6).

4. 1 Corinthians 12-14 . Paul taught concerning the gift of tongues. In his first letter to the Corinthians he mentioned tongues in his two listings of spiritual gifts (12:10, 28). He also spoke of "the tongues of men and of angels" (13:1). He further taught extensively concerning the proper use of the gift of tongues in public worship (14:11-33).

5. Romans 8:26. When in this verse Paul says that "the Spirit himself intercedes for us with groans that words cannot express," he is likely referring to the practice of praying in tongues (cf. 1 Cor. 14:14). Paul could have also been referring to other forms of Spirit-inspired prayer.

No honest student of the Bible can deny the fact that speaking in tongues is a biblical practice. The Bible teaches that speaking in tongues will continue as a practice in the church until second coming of Jesus (Acts 2:39; 1 Cor. 13:8-10).

Speaking in Tongues Defined

Let's now define speaking in tongues. We will do this by citing four scriptural truths about the practice:

1. A spiritual experience. Speaking in tongues is a experience with the Spirit of God. It is an experience common to Spirit-filled believers around the world. It occurs when the Spirit of God moves upon the spirit of a yielded disciple. Under the direction of the Spirit of God, he begins to speak in a language he has never learned (Acts 2:1-4).

2. A supernatural experience. Not only is speaking tongues a spiritual experience, it is also a supernatural experience. The Bible says that on the Day of Pentecost there came a sound "from heaven" like a blowing wind (Acts 2:2). This indicates that the disciples' experience on that day, which included speaking in tongues, had its origin in heaven. Paul described speaking in tongues as a "manifestation of the Spirit" (1 Cor. 12:7). In other words, speaking in tongues is a supernatural experience coming from the Spirit of God.

3. A real language. Third, speaking in tongues is a real language, not unintelligible gibberish, or "ecstatic speech," as it is incorrectly rendered in Goodspeed's translation.[1] It is a actual language. It can be in any human language or dialect, or it can be a heavenly language:

- *A human language.* On the Day of Pentecost the people

---

[1] Edgar Goodspeed, *The New Testament: An American Translation* (Chicago: University of Chicago Press, 1948).

heard the 120 speaking in their own native languages:
"Utterly amazed, they asked: 'Are not all these men who
are speaking Galileans? Then how is it that each of us
hears them in his own native language?'" (Acts 2:7-8).
They were speaking in known human languages.

- *A heavenly language.* Speaking in tongues can also be in
  a heavenly language. Paul taught that when a person is
  speaking in tongues he could be speaking in the "tongues
  of men" or "of angels" (1 Cor. 13:1).

4. A universal experience. Finally, speaking in tongues can
be described as a universal experience. That is, it is an experience
for all believers. Just as the baptism in the Holy Spirit is an
experience for all Christians (Acts 2:17-18, 39), its companion
experience, speaking in tongues, is also an experience for all
Christians. We say this for three reasons:

- Jesus said that tongues is a sign that can be expected to
  accompany "those who believe" (Mark 16:17).
- On the Day of Pentecost "all of them were filled with the
  Holy Spirit and began to speak in other tongues" (Acts
  2:4). Pentecost thus became the pattern for all
  generations of Christians (2:29).
- Paul told the Corinthian believers, "I would like every
  one of you to speak in tongues" (1 Cor. 14:5).

Every Christian should desire and expect to be filled with
the Spirit and to speak in tongues as the Spirit gives utterance.
Paul wrote to the Corinthian church saying, "What then shall we
say brothers? When you come together, everyone has a hymn, a

word of instruction, a revelation, a tongue or an interpretation. All of these must be done for the strengthening of the church" (1 Cor. 14:26). Notice that Paul said that, "everyone . . . has a tongue." This does not mean that everyone will speak a public message in tongues in every gathering of the church. It does imply, however, that any Spirit-filled believer can be used in this manner to edify the church as the Spirit wills.

SIX BENEFITS OF SPEAKING IN TONGUES IN PRIVATE DEVOTIONS

Now that we have defined speaking in tongues, we will answer the question, "Of what benefit is speaking in tongues?" In order to properly answer this question an explanation is needed. Scripturally, speaking in tongues can be divided into two broad categories: private tongues and public tongues. As such, prayer in tongues has both private and public functions. It also has both personal as well as corporate benefits.

We will first discuss how the spiritual life of an individual believer can be benefitted by praying in tongues. Here, we will not be talking about "messages in tongues" that are spoken in public worship services. (We will discuss that subject later in this chapter.) We will rather be talking primarily about prayer in tongues during a believer's private devotional time. This kind of prayer in tongues is sometimes referred to as one's "personal prayer language." The Bible speaks of six personal benefits of praying in tongues in this manner:

Builds One Up Spiritually

The first way prayer in tongues can benefit an individual believer is that, as he prays in tongues, he receives spiritual strength and blessing. Paul said, "He who speaks in a tongue edifies himself" (1 Cor. 14:4). In fact, speaking in tongues is the only spiritual gift about which the Bible specifically states that it edifies the person administering it. As one spends time before God praying in tongues, he receives spiritual strength.

Keeps One Conscious of the Presence

Another way that praying in tongues benefits the believer is by helping him or her to remain conscious of the presence of the Holy Spirit within. How important it is for every believer to be constantly aware of the indwelling presence of the Spirit. Such an awareness can be a source of great joy and confidence. Speaking of the Holy Spirit, Jesus promised His disciples, "He is with you and will be in you" (John 14:17). The Holy Spirit abides in the life of every true Christian (Rom. 8:9); however, many Christians must admit that they seldom really sense His indwelling presence. One remedy for this problem is prayer in the Spirit. As many Spirit-filled believers can testify, daily praying in tongues makes one more conscious of the Spirit dwelling inside.

Helps One Learn to More Fully Trust God

A third way that speaking in tongues benefits the individual believer is that it helps him or her learn to more fully trust God. This is because speaking in tongues is an act of faith and abandonment to God. In order to pray in the Spirit, one must yield himself to God and put his complete trust in Him. He must believe that God will guide his prayer. As the believer prays thus in the Spirit, he learns to more fully trust in God and His grace.

Eliminates Selfishness from Entering Our Prayers

Another way that praying in tongues benefits the believer's spiritual life is that it helps to eliminate selfishness from entering into his or her prayers. Try as we may, we cannot totally eliminate selfishness from our prayers. They inevitably turn inward to our own needs and concerns. All too often we forget the many needs of people around us and around the world. Here again, the Spirit helps us. As we yield ourselves to Him, He will pray through us "with groans that words cannot express" (Rom. 8:26). And He will pray according to the benevolent will of God (v. 27). As a result, our prayers will become, as were the prayers of Jesus, selfless and others-centered.

A Perfect Outlet for Praise and Worship

A fifth personal benefit of speaking in tongues is that it is a perfect outlet for praise and worship. The Spirit of God helps us in our worship of God by lifting our hearts to God (Rom. 8:15). Often He will take over our prayers, and worship God through us in tongues. Paul taught that the person who speaks in an unknown tongue is "praising God with [his] spirit" and giving thanks to Him (1 Cor. 14:16). Is it any wonder, then, that Paul exulted, "So what shall I do? I will pray with my spirit . . . I will sing with my spirit?" (v. 15). How wonderful it is to have the Holy Spirit come into our worship time and raise our spirits to God in praise and worship in a brand new tongue.[2]

---

[2] For a more thorough discussion of this subject see Chapter 12, "Worship in the Spirit."

The Scriptural Evidence of the Baptism in the Holy Spirit

There is another personal benefit of speaking in tongues we should mention before we finish this discussion. As we learned in Chapter 4, speaking in tongues is the first indication that a person has been baptized in the Holy Spirit. The truly Spirit-baptized believer need never doubt whether he has received the Holy Spirit. He doesn't need to blindly "take it by faith," as some have suggested. He knows that he has been filled with the Spirit because God has given him a beautiful new prayer language as evidence of his Spirit baptism.

THREE BENEFITS OF SPEAKING IN TONGUES IN PUBLIC WORSHIP

We have discussed six benefits of speaking in tongues to the personal life of the individual believer. We will now talk about three scriptural benefits of tongues in public worship. Note that we are now speaking of the tongues as a gift of the Holy Spirit (1 Cor. 12:10, 28) rather than tongues as a personal prayer language (1 Cor. 14:18-19) or as the evidence that one has been baptized in the Holy Spirit (Acts 2:4; 10:46).

The Gift of Tongues

In 1 Corinthians 14 Paul gives clear instructions concerning the benefits and uses of this wonderful gift in public worship. He says that it is always to be used with the gift of the interpretation of tongues (1 Cor. 14:5, 27). He further states that the primary purpose of this, as with all spiritual gifts, is to build up the church (1 Cor. 14:12, 26).

111

Three Benefits

When properly exercised, the gifts of tongues and the interpretation of tongues bring great blessing to a congregation. The exercise of the these twin gifts has three primary benefits:

1. Communicating divine truth. First, the gift of tongues, along with the gift of interpretation of tongues, is a God-ordained method of communicating divine truth to a congregation. Paul says that the gift of tongues, when followed by the gift of the interpretation of tongues, can be considered as a prophetic message to a congregation (1 Cor. 14:5). Through the tandem use of these gifts, God can communicate a prophetic word to a congregation of believers.

In 1 Corinthians 14:8 Paul compares speaking in tongues with interpretation to a battle trumpet calling a company of soldiers to battle. Then, in verse 21, he quotes the prophet Isaiah and says that God uses "strange tongues" to speak to his people (28:11-12). This use of the gift of tongues is what we commonly refer to in Pentecostal circles as a "message in tongues." When used with the gift of the interpretation of tongues, it is a powerful

way through which the Holy Spirit can communicate divine truth to a gathered body of believers.

2. Prophetic prayer. Not only can the gift of tongues function as a means of communicating divine truth *to* a congregation, it can also serve as a means of Spirit-directed prayer *for* the congregation. Note that Paul says when one is speaking in tongues, he is speaking primarily to God for "he does not speak to men but to God" (1 Cor. 14:2). He then says that such a prayer in tongues should be interpreted "so that the church may be edified" (v. 5).

While the typical Pentecostal church is familiar with "messages in tongues," whereby God speaks to a congregation through the gifts of tongues and interpretation, most Pentecostal congregations are not familiar with the gift of tongues as a Spirit-directed prayer on behalf of the congregation. This is tragic, especially since, according to Paul, this seems to be the primary use of the gift of tongues.

This use of the gift of tongues, which is sometimes called "prophetic prayer," functions much like a message in tongues. It is, however, not a message to the church, but a Spirit-directed prayer to God in an unknown tongue. Think of it. It is a prayer from the Spirit to God on our behalf! Like a message in tongues, it is interpreted into the language of the congregation. Imagine how a congregation can be blessed as it hears the Spirit Himself praying for them through the gifts of tongues and the interpretation of tongues.

We must insert a warning here. We do this because, when improperly used, tongues can also serve as a negative sign to unbelievers who come into our churches. When not used according to the guidelines set forth by Paul in 1 Corinthians 14, visitors to the church may even say that Spirit-filled Christians are out of their minds (v. 23). It is important, therefore, that we learn what the Bible teaches about the proper use of the gift of tongues. And it is equally important that we strictly follow those guidelines.[3]

---

[3] For an extended discussion on the proper used of tongues in public worship see the author's book *Power Ministry: How to Minister in the Spirit's Power,* chapter 8, "Pastoring the Spiritual

3. A sign that God is present. There is a third way that the gift of tongues can benefit a congregation. It can serve as a sign to unbelievers in the congregation that God is present in the midst of His people. Paul speaks of this use of the gift of tongues: "Tongues, then are a sign, not for believers, but for unbelievers" (1 Cor. 14:22). How can the gift of tongues serve as a sign for unbelievers? It can serve as a sign to unbelievers in two ways:

A trumpet call. First, when properly administered, the gift of tongues makes the unbeliever to know that God is present in the congregation, and that He is ready to speak to His people. Just as in ancient times a trumpet call signaled the fact that an important announcement was about to take place, tongues can be a signal to the unbeliever that something important and supernatural is taking place. The unbeliever is thus prepared to listen closely to the interpretation that follows.

A miraculous word. There is a second way tongues can serve as a sign to unbelievers. This happens when the speaker in tongues speaks in a language unknown to himself but known to

an unbeliever who is present in the congregation. It is a convincing sign of God's miraculous presence.

This is what happened on the Day of Pentecost. The people were amazed and wondered at the meaning of the disciples speaking in their own languages, which were unknown to the speakers (Acts 2:11-12). This gave Peter the opportunity to stand and explain to them what was happening (vv. 14-21). As a result

---

Gifts," published by Africa's Hope, Springfield, MO, USA.

many came to the Lord. In his book *Spoken By the Spirit,*[4] Ralph Harris has recorded many testimonies of those who, under the Spirit's inspiration, spoke in languages unknown to them but understood by foreign language speakers present.

———————————

Prayer in tongues, whether used in private devotions or in public worship, can bring tremendous spiritual blessing. We should not neglect the use of this wonderful gift from God. In our private devotions we should pray in the Spirit daily. In our church services we should welcome the proper use of the gift of tongues with interpretation.

———————————

[4] Ralph Harris, *Spoken By the Spirit: Documented Accounts of "Other Tongues" From Arabic to Zulu* (Springfield, MO: Gospel Publishing House, 1973).

- CHAPTER 9 -

OVERCOMING TEMPTATION

THROUGH THE POWER
OF THE SPIRIT

There is the story of the mother who caught four-year-old Johnny with his hand in the cookie jar. "Johnny," she pleaded, "why can't you just be good?" He answered, "Oh, mom, it makes me tired to be good." One way in which every believer struggles is in the area of temptation and sin. Let's face it, sometimes it just makes us tired to be good.

In this chapter we will discuss how the Spirit enables us to overcome temptation. We will first talk about temptation in general. Then, we will talk about how the Holy Spirit can give us victory over temptation and sin.

UNDERSTAND WHAT THE BIBLE SAYS ABOUT TEMPTATION

To win the battle over temptation, the believer must understand what the Bible teaches about the nature of temptation. There are five truths which we must all understand about temptation:

We Must All Cope with Temptation

It cannot be avoided. Temptation is a part of every person's life. Whether sinner or saint, no matter what age or station in life, everyone faces temptation. The Bible states clearly that "every man is tempted" (James 1:14, KJV). Even Jesus was tempted! (Matt. 4:1-11; 26:36-42; Heb. 4:15).

We must also realize, however, that being tempted is not in itself sin. Jesus was tempted, "yet without sin" (Heb. 4:15). One commits sin only when he lingers and yields to the temptation. One preacher said, "You cannot keep the birds from flying over your head, but you can keep them from nesting in your hair." In the same manner, we cannot keep temptations from coming our way, but we can keep from yielding to them.

Victory is Possible

A second truth we must understand about temptation is that it is possible to be victorious over temptation. God will always provide a way out of the temptation. Paul encouraged the Corinthian believers:

No temptation has seized you except what is common to man. And God is faithful; he will not let you be tempted beyond what you can bear. But when you are tempted, he will also provide a way out so that you can stand up under it. (1 Cor. 10:13)

In every temptation God offers us His power to overcome. We are not helpless puppets to Satan, nor or we slaves to our own fleshly lusts, but we can win the battle against temptation. Through the power of the Spirit we have been given "everything we need for life and godliness" (2 Pet. 1:3). By that same power we can win the battle against temptation and sin.

The Sources of Temptation

To triumph over temptation we must also understand something about the sources of temptation. The Bible teaches that there are three sources of temptation. One of these sources is from within the individual, the other two come from without. From within we are tempted by the lusts that spring from our own carnal nature. From without, we are tempted by the world and by evil spirits. It is through the power of the Holy Spirit that we are able to overcome each source of temptation. Let's discuss each of these three sources of temptation:

1. Our own carnal nature. Our first source of temptation is our own carnal natures. Every person has a carnal nature. The Bible teaches that we have all inherited this depraved, sinful nature from our forefather, Adam (Rom. 5:12). It is through this carnal nature that we are tempted to sin. As such, temptation comes from the inside. James wrote that "each one is tempted when, by his own evil desire, he is dragged away and enticed" (James 1:14). These temptations include "the cravings of sinful man, the lust of his eyes, and the boasting of what he has and does" (1 John 2:16).

Man's depraved nature is his natural inclination to sin. Jesus was speaking of humankind's depraved nature when He said,

> For from within, out of men's hearts, come evil thoughts, sexual immorality, theft, murder, adultery, greed, malice, deceit, lewdness, envy, slander, arrogance, and folly. All of these things come from inside and make a man "unclean." (Mark 7:21-23)

This depraved nature delights in rebelling against the laws of God (Rom. 8:7). It finds it very difficult and unnatural to do what is right and good.

2. The world. The Christian's second source of temptation is the world. Unlike temptation that comes from man's inner carnal nature, this temptation comes from the outside. When the Bible speaks of the world, it is often talking about this world's scheme of things. It is speaking of the systems and values of unregenerate society. These systems include the arts, the entertainment industry, commerce, politics, religion, and even educational systems. The Bible teaches that the whole world lies under the controlling influence of Satan (1 John 5:19). It is set against God.

John commands Christians, "Do not love the world or anything in the world. If anyone loves the world, the love of the Father is not in him" (1 John 2:15). And yet, we know that the world holds a great attraction for the natural man. Great temptations often come from our fascination with the things of the world.

3. Evil spirits. A third source of temptation for Christians is

119

evil spirits. We are again tempted from without by the devil and demons. In the Garden of Eden, Adam and Eve were tempted by the Serpent, Satan (Gen. 3:1-7; Rev. 20:2). In the New Testament Satan is called "the tempter" (Matt. 4:3; 1 Thess. 3:5). Just as Jesus was enticed by Satan in the wilderness to turn from His mission and commitment to God, we are also tempted by evil spirits to turn from God's mission and our commitment to that mission.

The Battlefield

Not only must the Christian understand the *sources* of temptation, he must also understand the *arena* of temptation. By this we mean that he must know where the battle for good and evil is fought. The believer must understand two things about this battle for his soul:

1. A mental battle. Today we hear much talk about spiritual warfare. It is talked about as if it is something that takes place somewhere "out there" in some distant spiritual realm. While there is some limited truth in this statement, it is only a small part of the truth. The vast majority of spiritual warfare is right now taking place in the hearts and minds of men and women. The Bible describes this spiritual warfare as follows:

> For though we live in the world, we do not wage war as the world does. The weapons we fight with are not the weapons of the world. On the contrary, they have divine power to demolish strongholds. We demolish arguments and every pretension that sets itself up against the knowledge of God, and we take captive every thought, to make it obedient to Christ. (2 Cor. 10:3-5)

Notice carefully that, in this verse, Paul identifies our minds as the arena where spiritual warfare takes place. It involves "thoughts," "arguments," and "pretensions." The battlefield is our own thought lives.

2. A spiritual battle. Not only is the battle against temptation a mental battle, it is also a spiritual battle. Paul said that "the weapons we fight with are not the weapons of the world" (2 Cor. 10:4). He went on to say that these weapons have "divine power." On another occasion Paul taught that our struggle "is not against flesh and blood, but against . . . spiritual forces of evil" (Eph. 6:12). Ours is a spiritual struggle. Our battle with temptation and sin will never be won if we use the weapons of this world. We must use the spiritual weapons that God provides.

Never Say, "I Can't Resist"

A final thing we must know about temptation is that, when a Christian is tempted, he or she can never truthfully say, "This temptation is too great for me. I cannot resist it." People undergoing temptation often complain. They accuse others, and sometimes even God. Nevertheless, according to James 1:13, and 1 Corinthians 10:13 there are four things that a Christian can never say when he is tempted:

1. "I am being tempted by God." When someone faces a temptation, he cannot point his finger at God and say, "God is the tempter." The reason is clear: "For God cannot be tempted by evil, nor does he tempt anyone" (James 1:13). If this is so, then where does the temptation come from? The Bible answers

this question: "Each one is tempted when, by his own evil desire, he is dragged away and enticed" (v. 14).

2. "I am the only one who has ever been tempted like this."

Often, when a person faces a severe temptation, he feels as if he is being tempted in a way that no other person has ever suffered. In his despair he is tempted to ask the question, "Why is God allowing me to be tempted this way? I am sure that no one else has ever being tempted like this!" But the Bible says that we should never make this statement because "no temptation has seized you except what is common to man" (1 Cor. 10:13).

Anytime we are tempted, we can know that others, somewhere in the world, are experiencing the same temptation, and through the power of the Spirit many are triumphing over it. We can, therefore, take courage knowing that, if they can overcome the temptation, so can we.

3. *"This temptation is too strong for me to resist."* Another thing a Christian must never say when he is being tempted is that the temptation is too great to resist. John declared, "The one who is in you is greater than the one who is in the world" (1 John 4:4). Paul encouraged the Corinthian believers, "God is faithful; he will not let you be tempted beyond what you can bear" (1 Cor. 10:13). God is watching over our souls. In His benevolent providence He will not allow any of us to be tempted in a way that we cannot resist.

4. *"There is no way out of this temptation but to yield to it."* A final thing that we cannot truthfully say when we face temptation is, "I must yield to this temptation; there is no other choice." The Bible says, "But when you are tempted, [God] will provide a way out so that you can stand up under it" (1 Cor. 10:13).

What then shall we conclude from these truths? We conclude that the battle with temptation is always winnable—if we will learn to live in step with the Spirit. This brings us to the second thing we must know about overcoming temptation.

WE MUST KNOW HOW THE SPIRIT HELPS US TRIUMPH OVER TEMPTATION

We now come to the most important part of this chapter, where we discuss some very practical steps one can take to win the battle over temptation. The Bible speaks of four tactics a Christian can employ to emerge victorious over temptation and sin:

Be Filled with the Spirit

The action that every Christian must take if he or she is to have victory over the world, the flesh, and the devil, is to be filled with the Spirit. The reader will note that we have already suggested this tactic in previous chapters. He should also know that we will suggest it again in the following chapters. This is because being filled with the Spirit is at the very heart of the Spirit-filled life.

Paul explained how the Holy Spirit helps us overcome temptation: "If you live according to the sinful nature, you will die; but if by the Spirit you put to death the misdeeds of the body, you will live" (Rom. 8:13). It is only through the power of the Spirit that we can have victory over temptation. Meditate carefully on the following Bible passages from the book of Galatians:

- "Live by the Spirit, and you will not gratify the desires

of the sinful nature" (5:16).

- "Those who belong to Christ Jesus have crucified the sinful nature with its passions and desires" (5:24).
- "Since we live by the Spirit, let us keep in step with the Spirit" (5:25).

You will notice that, in each case, Paul is saying that it is through the indwelling power of the Spirit that we are able to face and defeat temptation when it comes to us.

Avoid Temptation

A second very practical way to triumph over temptation is to simply avoid those things which tempt us to sin. Jesus taught us to pray, "Lead us not into temptation but deliver us from the evil one" (Matt. 6:13). Certainly, if we are going to ask God to not lead us into temptation, then we must ourselves seek to avoid the same. Paul instructed the Romans to "walk properly." Then he said, "Make no provision for the flesh to fulfill its lusts" (Rom. 13:13-14, NKJV). One sure way we can do this by avoiding temptations.

We are to stay away from those places where "the flesh has its fling" (cf. Rom. 13:14). This could include such places as bars, discos, and theaters. Paul instructed Timothy, his son in the faith, to "flee the evil desires of youth" (2 Tim. 2:22). Just as Joseph fled from the sexual advances of Potiphar's wife (Gen. 39:7-12), we must flee every appearance of evil (1 Thess. 5:22). David prayed, "I will be careful to lead a blameless life . . . I will walk in my house with a blameless heart. I will set before my eyes no vile thing" (Ps. 101:2-4). We too, if we are going to be victorious over temptation and sin, must not set any vile thing before our eyes. This includes pornographic books and magazines, lewd music and videos, and unclean television programs.

Clothe Yourself in Christ

Making no provision for the sinful nature is one way we can overcome temptation. Another is to clothe ourselves with the Lord Jesus Christ. Listen to Paul's words: "Clothe yourselves with the Lord Jesus Christ, and do not think about how to gratify the desires of the sinful nature" (Rom. 13:14).

According to verse 12 of the same chapter, to clothe oneself in Jesus is to "put on the armor of light." In Ephesians 6 this armor of light is called the "full armor of God" (vv. 11, 13). If you will put on this armor, you will be able to "take your stand against the devil's schemes" (v. 11). Then, "when the evil day comes you will be able to stand your ground" (v. 13). This armor of the Spirit includes truth, righteousness, preparedness, faith, salvation, the Word of God, and prayer in the Spirit. As the Spirit-filled Christian clothes himself in this armor, and thus in the character of Christ, he will be able to stand against any temptation.

Learn the Secret of Resisting and Yielding

A final tactic for overcoming temptation is the spiritual tactic of "resisting and yielding." Before we discuss this powerful tactic for overcoming temptation, it will be helpful if we first look at what happens when a Christian yields to temptation and commits sin. When faced with a temptation, the Christian will always have to make two bad choices in order to give in to that temptation and commit sin: First, he will have to yield himself to the temptation. Secondly, he will have to resist the promptings of the Holy Spirit.

Because the Holy Spirit dwells within him, the Spirit-filled Christian will always have to resist the Spirit before he can sin. This is because the Spirit will be constantly vigilant, urging to him to avoid the sin (John 16:8-11). Therefore, before a believer can sin, he will have to both yield to the temptation and resist the Holy Spirit.

But the reverse is also true. In order to overcome the temptation, the Christian will have to do just the opposite of what he had to do in order to sin (see chart below.) To sin, he had to yield to the temptation, now, in order to overcome, he must resist the temptation. In like manner, in order to sin, he had to resist the Holy Spirit, now in order to overcome the temptation, he will have to yield to the Holy Spirit.

To Sin **A Christian Must . . .**	**To Overcome** **A Christian Must . . .**
Yield to the temptation	Resist the temptation
Resist the Spirit	Yield to the Spirit

When used together, these two spiritual tactics, resisting and yielding, are a powerful, unbeatable team against any temptation to sin. Let's look more closely at each of these tactics:

1. Resisting. First, in order to overcome temptation, the

Christian must firmly resist the temptation. We all understand resisting. It is a conscious freewill choice that we make *not* to do something. It is an act of inner self control. Such self control is one of the fruit of the Spirit-filled life (Gal. 5:23). When a temptation from the devil comes, we must steadfastly resist it (1 Pet. 5:9).

Although resisting temptation is essential, it is not enough. Paul vividly describes the futility of trying to resist temptation in one's own strength in Romans 7:18-25. There he describes the frustration of constant failure when he says, "For I have the desire to do what is good, but I cannot carry it out" (v. 18). Resist we must, but it is not enough!

2. Yielding. This brings us to the second, and more powerful, tactic for overcoming temptation—the tactic of yielding to the Spirit. As mentioned above, when a Christian faces temptation, the Holy Spirit is there to convict him and encourage him to do what is right. In order to overcome the temptation the Christian must now begin to yield himself to these inner promptings of the Spirit. No matter how small or insignificant they may seem, he must consciously yield himself to them.

The temptation may loom large and powerful, and the voice of the Spirit may seem small and faint. What is the bewildered believer to do in such a case? *He must turn to the Spirit!* He must yield himself to the Spirit's inner urgings. As he does this, he will, at the same time, turn his back on the temptation. At such a time he may want to pray in the Spirit. As he yields himself to the power of the Spirit, the power of the temptation becomes weaker.

James said, "Resist the devil, and he will flee from you.

127

Draw near to God and He will draw near to you" (4:7-8). In order to overcome temptation we must do both. We must resist the devil, but we must, at the same time, draw near to God.

When we do this, a powerful principle takes over. This principle is called "the law of the Spirit of life" (Rom. 8:2). Through this powerful principle we are set free from the law of sin and death. Read more about the working of this powerful principle in Romans 8:1-9. Paul describes this process of resisting and yielding:

> Therefore do not let sin reign in your mortal body so that you obey its evil desires. Do not offer the parts of your body to sin, as instruments of wickedness, but rather offer yourselves to God as those who have been brought from death to life; and offer the parts of your body to him as instruments of righteousness . . . I put this in human terms because you are weak in your natural selves. Just as you used to offer the parts of your body in slavery to impurity and to ever-increasing wickedness, so now offer them in slavery to righteousness leading to holiness. (Rom. 6:12-13, 19)

Paul is reminding the Roman Christians of their past lives before they knew Christ. He is telling them to remember how they had once yielded to temptation, and how they had yielded their bodies to sin (Rom. 6:19). He is saying that they should now do just the opposite. Instead of yielding to sin, as they had done in the past, they should now yield themselves to God. They should yield themselves to the inner urgings of the Holy Spirit. This will lead to righteous living.

Before closing this section on yielding to the Spirit, we make two important observations: First, we reemphasize the importance of every Christian being filled with the Holy Spirit.

The Christian who is not full of the Spirit will have little strength in resisting the temptations of the devil and the pull of the flesh. The Bible is clear on this point: "Walk in the Spirit and you will not fulfill the lusts of the flesh" (Gal. 5:16).

Secondly, we stress the importance of the Christian's learning how to yield himself to the Spirit. This practice is best learned in a Spirit-filled worship service. Often in such an atmosphere, the Holy Spirit will move on the Christian and prompt him to do something. This could be to repent of a sin, dedicate himself more fully to Christian service, or to release a spiritual gift. As the Christian obeys the voice of the Spirit, he learns how to more fully yield himself to the Spirit. Then, as he goes out of the church service into the world, he is more prepared to yield to the Spirit when he is tempted.

But if, in the church service, he is in the habit of resisting the promptings of the Spirit, he is likely to resist the Spirit when temptation comes. And he is likely to be overcome by the temptation. How important it is for us to learn to respond to the voice of the Spirit of God.

Temptations will come into the Christian's life, but when they come the Spirit-filled Christian can be victorious. Through the power of the Spirit we can triumph over every temptation!

CHAPTER 10

GUIDANCE
INTO ALL TRUTH

The preacher droned on and on, or should I say, he ranted on and on? He was clearly full of himself and not full of the Spirit. Worse of all, he was twisting the Scriptures, making them to say something neither the Holy Spirit nor the original writer had in mind when the text was first inspired and written. I was saddened as the people sat listening to this clear mis-representation of truth.

Nothing in the Christian life is so important as a proper understanding and application of the teachings of God's Word. False religions have been started, and many sincere seekers after truth have been led astray, because of someone's mis-interpretation of Scripture. This is one issue with which every gospel worker must concern himself. He must properly interpret and communicate of the true teachings of the Bible.

In this chapter we will discuss how the Holy Spirit helps us to understand and interpret the Word of God. We will discuss three issues concerning the role of the Spirit and the Word in the Christian life: (1) the importance of the Word of God to the Spirit-filled life, (2) the importance of the Spirit in understanding

and applying the Word to our lives, and (3) how
to properly approach the Word of God.

THE IMPORTANCE OF THE WORD TO THE SPIRIT-FILLED LIFE

The Spirit-filled life cannot be divorced from the Word of
God. Anyone who tries to do so is very foolish indeed. The Word
and the Spirit go together. Understanding and obeying the Bible
is at the very heart of the Spirit-filled life. There are three ways
that the Word of God is very important to the Spirit-filled life:

The Revealer of the Spirit-Filled Life

First, the Word of God is important to the Spirit-filled life
because it is the revealer of the Spirit-filled life. In its pages we
learn about the Holy Spirit and His working in our lives. In fact,
without the Bible we would have no authoritative knowledge at
all about the Spirit of God. We would be ignorant concerning the
Spirit-filled life, its benefits, or how it is to be lived. It is through
studying God's Word that we understand these truths.

Do you want to know more about life in the Spirit? Then,
apply yourself to the Word. The Bible is indeed the revealer of
the Spirit-filled life.

The Guide for the Spirit-filled Life

Further, the Bible is important to the Spirit-filled walk
because it is our only authoritative guide on how to live a life in
step with the Spirit. Just as a master builder will use a detailed
blueprint to build a beautiful cathedral, the Spirit-filled believer

132

uses the Bible as his or her guide for Spirit-filled living. This is why we have been very careful to ensure that all the truths taught in this book are based squarely on the Word of God.

If any teaching is not supported by the Word of God, we should question it. If it is substantiated by the Word, we must obey it. The Scriptures say about the believers in Berea that "they were of more noble character than the Thessalonians, for they received the message with eagerness and examined the Scriptures every day to see if what Paul said was true" (Acts 17:11). We too, every time we hear a teaching about the things of the Spirit, we must ask the question, "Is this teaching firmly supported by God's Word?" If it is, we must embrace it. If it isn't, we must reject it.

The "Umpire" for the Spirit-filled Life

The Word of God is important to a life in the Spirit for another reason. The Bible serves as the "umpire" for the Spirit-filled life. Just as a umpire watches over a baseball game to make certain that all of the players are playing by the rules, the Word of God will watch over our spiritual lives to ensure that we are playing by God's rules.

We often hear people say, "The Spirit told me to do this or that." And at times, we hear the voice of the Spirit ourselves. What are we to do on such occasions? The Bible gives the answer: We are to test the spirits (1 John 4:1). But how do we test them? One sure method is by asking the question, "Does this 'word' square with the Word of God?" In a baseball game the ball must be kept in bounds. If at anytime a batter hits the ball out of bounds, the umpire will shout, "Foul ball!" The Bible can serve the same function in the life of the Spirit-filled believer. It can tell him when his "word" from the Lord is fair or foul. Many have gone astray because they have not submitted themselves to the authority of God's Word. We must never make that tragic mistake.

THE SPIRIT WILL HELP US TO UNDERSTAND THE WORD

One important way that the Spirit aids us in our spiritual lives is by helping us to understand Scripture. The Word of God can be accurately understood only by those in right relationship with the Holy Spirit, for the Bible says, "The man without the Spirit does not accept the things that come from the Spirit of God, for they are foolishness to him, and he cannot understand them, because they are spiritually discerned" (1 Cor. 2:14).

On the evening of His resurrection Jesus opened the minds of His disciples "so that they could understand the Scriptures" (Luke 24:45). In the same way the Holy Spirit, whom the Father has sent in Jesus' name, will open our minds to better understand the Scriptures (John 14:26). The Spirit is able to help us understand the Scriptures for at least three reasons:

The Author of the Word

The first reason why the Holy Spirit is able to help us interpret the Word of God is because He is its Author. The Bible teaches that it was the Holy Spirit who inspired the Word of God. Paul said, "All Scripture is God-breathed . . ." Peter told how this took place: "Above all, you must understand that no prophecy of Scripture came about by the prophet's own interpretation. For

134

prophecy never had its origin in the will of man, but men spoke from God as they were carried along by the Holy Spirit" (2 Pet. 1:20-21). These verses teach us three things about the inspiration of Scripture:

- *Scripture did not originate in the mind of man:* "No prophecy of Scripture came about by the prophet's own interpretation" (v. 21).
- *Scripture did not originate in the will of man:* "Prophecy never had its origin in the will of man" (v. 22a).
- *Scripture has its origin in the Holy Spirit:* "Men spoke from God as they were carried along by the Holy Spirit" (v. 22b).

Paul wrote the Corinthians about how God revealed the New Testament Scriptures to the apostles: "We have not received the spirit of the world but the Spirit who is from God, that we may understand what God has freely given us. This is what we speak, not in words taught us by human wisdom but in words taught by the Spirit . . ." (1 Cor. 2:12-13). As we read the Bible we can, therefore, be assured that we are not reading "words taught to us by human wisdom" but "words taught by the Spirit." The Spirit is, in truth, the Author of Scripture.

The Illuminator of the Word

The second reason why the Holy Spirit can help us understand the Bible is because He is the Illuminator of the Word. He is not only the divine Author of the Word, He is the divine Teacher of its sacred truths. Jesus promised, "But when he, the Spirit of truth, comes, He will guide you into all truth" (John 16:13). John wrote, "His anointing teaches you about all things" (1 John 2:27). As Spirit-filled believers, we can confidently look to the Holy Spirit to illuminate Scripture to us.

Theologians make an important difference between the concepts of inspiration and illumination. When they speak of inspiration they are speaking of the Holy Spirit's work in the prophets and apostles in revealing the Scriptures to them. We do not look for such inspiration today. The Bible is forever settled in heaven (Ps. 119.89). No more Scripture will be revealed or written. However, the Holy Spirit will be with us today illuminating the Scripture. He will help us to understand and rightly divide the Word of God.

Suppose that two men were arguing over the meaning of a verse of poetry. One man says it means one thing, the other says it means another. How best can their argument be settled? The best way that their argument could be settled is by asking the poet about the true meaning of the verse. Only he can give them the absolutely correct interpretation. In the same way, if we lack understanding about a verse of Scripture, we can go directly to its Author and Illuminator, the Holy Spirit, and He will help us to understand the true meaning.

Does this mean that we no longer need to use sound hermeneutical principles in interpreting the Word? No, it does not. In fact, just the opposite is true. Because of his relationship with the Holy Spirit, the Spirit-filled believer has a great love and respect for the Word of God. Therefore, he will be even more careful as to how he interprets the Word. He will seek illumination from the Holy Spirit, but at the same time, he will apply sound principles of biblical interpretation.

The Applier of the Word

A third reason why the Holy Spirit is able to help us understand the Bible is because He is the Applier of the Word of God. Not only will the Spirit illuminate the Word *for* us, He will also personalize the Word *to* us, and apply it's truths to our hearts. Jesus said of the Holy Spirit, "He will take of what is mine and declare it to you" (John 16:14-15). Many Spirit-filled Christians have testified about how the Spirit helped them when they were enduring a great trial of their faith, or facing a great decision in life. As they were reading the Word, the Holy Spirit took that Word and applied it directly to their situation. If we are to hear the Lord's voice in this manner, we must spend much time in prayerful reading and studying the Word of God.

HOW TO APPROACH THE
WORD OF GOD

If we are to receive the greatest benefit from the Word of God, we must know how to properly approach it. What should our attitude be as we approach the Bible? When we approach the Scriptures we should do so in the following four ways:

In Love and Humility

First, we should approach the Word of God in a spirit of love and humility. The Psalmist wrote, "I will lift up my hands to your commands, which I love . . ." (Ps. 119:48). Like him, the Spirit-filled Christian must have a deep and sincere love for the Word of God. Paul wrote the Christians in Thessalonica, "And we also thank God continually because, when you received the

Word of God, which you heard from us, you accepted it not as the word of men, but as it actually is, the Word of God" (1 Thess. 2:13).

We too must esteem the Bible as the actual words of God. We love the Word because it is an intimate revelation of the God whom we love and serve.

The Spirit-filled Christian will also approach the Bible in a spirit of humility. Rather than speaking to the Bible, he will let the Bible speak to him. He will not attempt to twist the Scriptures to fit his own pet doctrine or to justify his own sinful practices.

Sadly, far too many professed Pentecostal preachers and teachers treat the Word of God very carelessly. They try to make it say things that it does not really say. This is wrong, and God will judge anyone who treats His Word in such a manner (2 Pet. 3:16).

In a Spirit of Prayer

Not only must we approach the Word of God in a spirit of love and humility, we must also approach it in a spirit of prayer. Those to whom God originally revealed His word were in such a spirit of prayer. John wrote, "On the Lord's Day, I was in the Spirit . . ." (Rev. 1:10). It was in such a state of prayer that the Holy Spirit revealed to him the book of Revelation. We too, if we are going to properly interpret the Bible, must be in the Spirit. We must sincerely pray for God's insight and guidance each time we sit down to study the Word of God.

With Great Reverence and Caution

When we come to the Word of God, we must come with great reverence and caution. We must realize that there is the constant danger of our reading our own thoughts into the Bible. This can be very dangerous. Peter spoke of "those who are untaught and unstable" who " twist [the Scriptures] to their own destruction . . ." (2 Pet. 3:17, NKJV). We must reverence the Word of God so much that we will never treat it frivolously. To do so can result in our own destruction and the destruction of the people to whom we minister. At the very least, when we misinterpret and misapply Scripture, we are depriving ourselves, and God's people, of hearing the true Word of God.

With a Heart Open to the Voice of the Spirit

Finally, we must approach the Word of God with our hearts open to the voice of the Spirit. As we read the Bible, the Holy Spirit will speak to us. He will show us things in our lives that are not pleasing to God. He will reveal to us the answers to our problems and concerns. He will give us inspiration and encouragement. He will also show us certain truths that He wants us to preach or teach about. But, in order for the Lord to speak to us through His Word, we must read it with our hearts open to the voice of the Spirit. As we read the Bible, our constant prayer must be, "Speak Lord, for your servant is listening" (cf. 1 Sam. 3:10).

One of the great benefits of living a life in step with the Spirit is that the Spirit of God will help us to understand and apply the Word of God. We must constantly pray and submit ourselves to the Spirit as we read and interpret the Scriptures. If we will do this He will come and help to guide us into all truth.

CHAPTER 11

INTERCESSORY PRAYER
IN THE SPIRIT

I was seventeen and a senior in high school. It was a few weeks before I would give my life to Christ. One chilly Saturday morning in December of 1963 my employer had dropped me off at the First Assembly of God in Pasadena, Texas. I was working for him as a part-time janitor. My assignment for the day was to clean the Sunday school and office wing of the church. I immediately set myself to the task.

As I worked my way through the building, I began to hear deep groaning sounds coming from the office area at the far end of the building. Curious, I eased my way down the hall. The groaning sounds became louder. Finally, I came to a door marked "Pastor." It was opened just barely. As I peeked in, I saw a man kneeling at his chair. He was praying, and his prayer was in tongues. I was later to learn that the man was J. R. Goodwin, pastor of the church.

At the time, I did not understand what was happening, but I sensed that it was a holy moment. I quietly backed away from the door and went back to my work; however, an indelible impression was imprinted on my mind. It was years later before I fully understood the meaning of what was happening. I had come upon Pastor Goodwin as he was interceding in the Spirit.

As you may remember, in Chapter 2 we briefly mentioned the intercessory use of prayer in tongues. In this chapter we will expand our discussion about this kind of prayer in the Spirit. In doing this we will address three issues: (1) what is meant by the term "prayer in the Spirit," (2) how prayer in the Spirit blesses the one doing the intercessory praying, and (3) how such intercessory prayer in the Spirit blesses others.

PRAYER IN THE SPIRIT

Before we can properly discuss intercessory prayer in the Spirit, it will be well for us to first define the New Testament use of this term. Just what do we mean when we use the term prayer in the Spirit? When the Bible speaks of prayer in the Spirit, it uses the term in one of two ways:

Any Prayer That is Prompted by the Spirit

Generally speaking, prayer in the Spirit can be any prayer that is prompted and directed by the Spirit of God. When an anointing of the Spirit comes upon a Spirit-filled believer to initiate, prompt, and direct his prayers, this could be properly called prayer in the Spirit. Paul speaks of such prayer in Rom. 8:26-27:

> In the same way, the Spirit helps us in our weaknesses. We do not know what we ought to pray for, but the Spirit himself intercedes for us with groans that words cannot express. And he who searches our hearts knows the mind of the Spirit.

because the Spirit intercedes for us in accordance with God's will.

Such prayer is prayer in the Spirit because it is prayer that is initiated and directed by the Holy Spirit. Think about what Paul said in this verse: "The Spirit helps us . . . the Spirit intercedes for us."

Prayer in the Spirit is a cooperative effort between a Spirit-filled individual and Spirit Himself. The Holy Spirit directs and prompts the prayer, the Spirit-filled intercessor yields and cooperates. Thus, when one prays a "prophetic prayer" in tongues,[1] or interprets the same, he or she is praying in the Spirit.

At times the Spirit-filled Christian is prompted by the Holy Spirit to pray for a certain need. As he is praying for that need, the Holy Spirit may come powerfully upon him and anoint and direct his prayer. At such a time the believer is praying in the Spirit. Sometimes he will pray in his own language, and sometimes he may pray in tongues, which brings us to our second definition of prayer in the Spirit.

Prayer in Tongues

More specifically, when the Bible speaks of prayer in the Spirit, it is speaking of prayer in tongues. Paul viewed prayer in tongues and prayer in the Spirit as the same thing. In writing to the Corinthian church he said, "For anyone who speaks in a tongue, does not speak to men but to God. Indeed, no one understands him; he utters mysteries with his spirit" (1 Cor. 14:2).

---

[1] See Chapter 8 for an explanation of prophetic prayer.

Note that Paul said that anyone who "speaks in a tongue" is speaking "mysteries with his spirit." Some translators translate the phrase "with his spirit" as "in the Spirit." Paul further wrote,

> For if I pray in a tongue, my spirit prays, but my mind is unfruitful. So what shall I do? I will pray with my spirit, but I will also pray with my mind; I will sing with my spirit, but I will also sing with my mind. (vv. 14-15)

In these verses Paul mentions two kinds of prayer: prayer with the spirit and prayer with the mind, or understanding. In the chart below we compare these two kinds of prayer:

Two Kinds of Prayer Compared (1 Cor. 14:2, 14)	
Prayer in the Spirit	**Prayer with the Mind**
Our spirit prays (v. 14)	Our mind prays
Prayer in tongues (vv. 2, 14)	Prayer in a known language
We do not understand what we are saying (vv. 2, 14)	We understand what we are saying

Many Bible scholars believe that the "groans that words cannot express" spoken of in Romans 8:26 is prayer in tongues. Paul is describing prayer that is beyond human ability. He speaks of Spirit-prompted utterances. This verse is almost certainly making reference to the same prayer in tongues spoken of in 1 Corinthians 14:2, 14.

HOW INTERCESSORY PRAYER IN THE SPIRIT BLESSES THE ONE PRAYING

When praying in the Spirit, the intercessor receives great help from the Holy Spirit. As the Spirit prays through him, He prays with great power and effectiveness. As a result, the intercessor's own spiritual life is strengthened. The Bible speaks of three ways that prayer in the Spirit strengthens the one praying. Paul speaks of one way, and Jude speaks of two others.

Paul Spoke of One Benefit of Prayer in the Spirit

In 1 Corinthians 14:4 Paul spoke of a wonderful blessing that comes to the one who prays in the Spirit. He said, "He who speaks in a tongue edifies himself." This means that, as a person prays in tongues, he is built up in his spiritual life.

Surprisingly, some have sought to use this very verse as an argument against Christians praying in tongues. They say that it is wrong and selfish to pray in tongues, since in doing so, one only edifies himself. We must realize, however, that, before one can be a blessing to others, he must first allow God to bless him. We must appropriate the Spirit's strength before we can help others.

We could also truthfully say, "He who reads the Bible edifies himself." Is it, therefore, wrong to read the Bible? Should we prohibit people from reading the Bible simply because they are only blessing themselves? No, we should not, because in blessing themselves they are preparing themselves to bless others. And neither should we prohibit them from praying in tongues. This is one reason why Paul commanded, "Do not forbid speaking in tongues" (1 Cor. 14:39).

In Ephesians 6:18 Paul wrote, "Pray in the Spirit on all occasions with all kinds of prayers and requests." Great spiritual strength comes into the life of the Christian when he or she prays in the Spirit. Like the apostle Paul, we must boldly affirm, "I will pray with my spirit" (1 Cor. 14:14).

Jude Spoke of Two Benefits of Prayer in the Spirit

Jude spoke of two additional blessings that come to the one who is prays in the Spirit: "But you, beloved, building yourselves up on your most holy faith, praying in the Holy Spirit, keep yourselves in the love of God . . ." (vv. 20-21, NKJV). Here, Jude gives two specific ways one is edified by praying in the Spirit:

1. Faith is increased. The first blessing that comes from prayer in the Spirit is that our faith is increased. Note howat Jude indicated that we can build ourselves up "on our most holy faith" by praying in the Spirit. In Chapter 8 we discussed how prayer in tongues helps a person learn to more fully trust God. This is certainly wonderful; however, as a Christian spends time praying in the Spirit, an even more wonderful thing is happening. As he prays for others, God supernaturally imparts faith into his own life.

There is another way that prayer in the Spirit can serve to increase the faith of the intercessor. As one prays in the Spirit, he prays "in accordance with God's will" (Rom. 8:27). Since he is praying according to the will of God, it is inevitable that his prayers will be answered (1 John 5:14-15). As the intercessor sees his prayers answered, his faith is increased.

146

Here then is yet another reason why we should "pray in the Spirit on all occasions." Prayer in the Spirit is a powerful spiritual exercise whereby the believer becomes stronger and stronger in his faith in God and His Word.

2. *Kept in the love of God.* A third blessing that comes from intercessory prayer in tongues is that the one praying in the Spirit is "kept in the love of God." Jude says, "Praying in the Holy Spirit, keep yourselves in the love of God." Paul tells us that "God has poured out his love into our hearts by the Holy Spirit, who he has given us" (Rom. 5:5). As the Spirit-filled believer prays for others in tongues, he experiences the love of God. He draws near to God, and God draws near to him (James 4:8). As this happens, his love and consecration to God grows stronger.

HOW INTERCESSORY PRAYER IN THE SPIRIT BLESSES OTHERS

While the believer who intercedes for others in the Spirit receives blessing in his or her own spiritual life, this is not the primary purpose of intercessory prayer in the Spirit. Its main purpose is to bless others. Paul said that, as the Spirit prays through the intercessor, He "intercedes for the saints" (Rom. 8:27). In this way the Spirit prays through the Spirit-filled believer for the needs of others. Let's look more closely at Romans 8:26-27 and see how this intercession for others works. In these verses the apostle taught two things about our prayers:

How We Struggle in Prayer

Paul said that we all have a weakness in our prayer lives. He said, "We do not know what we ought to pray for" (Rom. 8:26). How many urgent needs do we fail to pray for simply because we are unaware of them? Even when we do know what to pray for, we often do not know exactly how to pray. This is because we often do not know God's will in the matter. And all too often, as discussed in Chapter 8, we pray with the wrong motives. Or, even worse, we simply lack any motivation at all to pray for others. We truly need the Spirit's help in our prayer lives.

How the Spirit Helps Us

At such times the Holy Spirit will come to our aid. Paul says, "The Spirit himself intercedes for us" (v. 26). As we yield ourselves to the Spirit of God, He will pray through us "with groans that words cannot express" (v. 27), that is, in words given to us by the Holy Spirit.

A closer look at Romans 8:26-27 reveals five powerful ways the Spirit helps us in prayer:

1. He "makes intercession for us." As we yield ourselves to the Holy Spirit, He comes to us, fills us with His power and presence, and prays through us. It is no longer us directing our own prayers, it is the Holy Spirit praying through us. What powerful way to pray!

2. He does this "with groans which words cannot express." As the Spirit moves in us, and we yield ourselves to Him, He will pray through us in words and phrases which He inspires. He begins to speak to God through us in expressions of His own creation.

3. He "searches our hearts." As we pray in the Spirit, the Holy Spirit will search the motives of our hearts and purify us through His sanctifying power (Rom. 8:1-8). As we yield to His power and presence, our hearts are cleansed from impure ways and motives (Ps. 51:10-11). As a result, we are placed in a position where God can answer our prayers (Isa. 59:1).

4. He "knows the mind of the Spirit." The Spirit of God knows perfectly the mind and will of God in any given matter (1 Cor. 2:11). Therefore, the prayer that He prays through us will be in accordance with God's perfect will.

5. He "intercedes for the saints according to the will of God." As we allow the Holy Spirit to pray through us, we will be praying for the needs of others, *and* we will be praying in God's perfect will. John teaches that God hears and answers prayers that are prayed in accordance with His will (1 John 5:14-15). Such prayers have great spiritual power.

The author himself can testify how on many occasions he has experienced such prayer in the Spirit. As the Spirit prayed through him in a language he had never learned, his life was blessed and strengthened. On some of these occasions he did not know who, or what, he was praying for. He only knew that the Holy Spirit was using him as His vessel to pray for someone in need. On other occasions, he knew who he was praying for, but he was not personally aware of any need in this person's life. On yet other occasions, he knew the person's need, but he was not certain of God's will in the matter. As he allowed the Holy Spirit to pray through him for the person in need, he knew that he was praying in the will of God.

Intercessory prayer in the Spirit has been a great blessing in my life. It can be a great blessing in the life of every Christian. We should never allow pride or spiritual laziness cause us to neglect this marvelous privilege of prayer in the Spirit.

Chapter 12

WORSHIP

IN THE SPIRIT

The Westminister Catechism reads, "Man's chief end is to glorify God, and to enjoy him for ever." Karl Barth once wrote, "Christian worship is the most momentous, the most urgent, the most glorious action that can take place in human life."[1] If all of this is true, then it must also be true that worship, being so important to the Christian life, must be done properly. In our last chapter we discussed how the Holy Spirit can help us in intercessory prayer. It this chapter we will discuss how He will help us to properly worship God.

THE ESSENCE OF TRUE WORSHIP

As we have discovered through the lessons in this book, the Christian life must be lived in step with the Spirit of God. This is especially true for worship. The only way one can properly

---

[1] J. J. Von Allmen, *Worship: Its Theology and Practice* (London: Lutterworth, 1965), 13; quoted in Ralph P. Martin, *The Worship of God* (Grand Rapids: Wm. B. Eerdmans, 1982), 1.

worship God is to worship Him in the Spirit. Let's look more closely at this important spiritual principle.

God Must Be Worshiped in Spirit

At hand-dug well in a remote dusty village in ancient Samaria Jesus gave to the world His greatest revelation concerning the nature of true worship. He said, "A time is coming and has now come when true worshipers will worship the Father in spirit and truth, for they are the kind of worshipers the Father seeks. God is spirit, and his worshipers must worship in spirit and in truth" (John 4:23-24). In this text, Jesus revealed four profound truths about essence of true worship:

- *God is spirit.* God is, by His very nature, spiritual. This means that He neither has, nor is He limited by, a physical form. He is, therefore, not bound to a single locale or time frame but can be worshiped in any place at any time.
- *God is seeking true worshipers.* God is looking for people who will worship Him according to His true nature. He no longer wants our worship to be characterized by outward form, but by inner devotion and sincerity.
- *True worship must be done in Spirit and in truth.* Since God is spiritual, those who worship Him must worship Him in Spirit. Since God is absolute truth, they must worship Him in truth.
- *It is now time for such worship.* The time to worship God in Spirit and in truth is now.

Jesus was saying to the woman at the well that God is

demanding of His people a new kind of worship. This new worship will no longer be based on ritual and ceremony. Nor will it be limited to a certain race of people or certain holy sites. God is now demanding that He be worshiped out of the heart, and under the direction of the Holy Spirit. This new kind of worship must be spiritual, involving the spirit of man reaching out to God. And it must be based on a truly loving relationship with God.

The Meaning of the Term "Worship in the Spirit"

When Jesus said that God must be worshiped "in spirit" (Gk: *en pneumati*), what did He mean? Biblical scholars have noted that the phrase "in spirit" in this passage can mean either in the Holy Spirit or with the human spirit.[2] In Scripture, the word spirit is used to speak of the Holy Spirit, the spirit of man, or the inner attitudes of man. Each time a biblical translator encounters this phrase, he must, based on his own understanding of the context, decide whether to use an uppercase "S" or a lowercase "s." Some commentators believe that in John 4:23-24 Jesus is referring to the human spirit and is talking about worship from the heart of man.[3] Others believe that He is speaking of the Spirit of God.[4] Whichever way this phrase is translated, a careful examination of Scripture indicates that both are concepts are

---

[2] Ralph W. Harris, ed.., *Complete Biblical Commentary,* "John," (Springfield, MO: World Library Press, 1989), 97.

[3] J. Rodman Williams, *Renewal Theology,* III, (Grand Rapids: Zondervan, 1992), 107.

[4] Stanley Horton, *What the Bible Says About the Holy Spirit* (Springfield, MO: Gospel Publishing House, 1976), 117.

valid. Let's look at each of these concepts:

1. Worship from our spirits. To worship in spirit (lowercase "s") means that we worship God out of our hearts, in total sincerity and honesty. True worship involves our human spirits reaching out in love and faith to God, whose is Himself, by very nature, spirit. True worship is not based on dead ritual but on a living relationship between a person and God. It is not done with inanimate objects but with a living, devoted human spirit (Ezek. 36:26-27).

2. Worship in His Spirit. Worship in Spirit (uppercase "S") speaks of worship that is prompted and energized by the Spirit of God. Paul reminded the Philippian believers that we "worship by the Spirit of God" (Phil. 3:3); that is, we are to let the Spirit of God initiate and energize our worship. In Luke's gospel we read of how both Mary and Zacharias were prompted by the Holy Spirit to speak wonderful words of praise (1:46-55; 67-79). On one occasion Jesus Himself was filled "with joy through the Holy Spirit" and began to praise His Heavenly Father (10:21). When Jesus said that we must worship God "in Spirit" He was saying that God cannot be truly worshiped apart from the help of the Holy Spirit. Bob Sorge wrote concerning the Spirit's role in worship:

> Jesus was further showing that our worship would one day be greatly enhanced through the fullness of the Holy Spirit. One beautiful reason why Jesus gave us the Holy Spirit, together with the gift of speaking in tongues, is that we might be released in a greater measure in our worship. There is a certain element in worship that will always be absent for those who do not accept the fullness of the Holy Spirit, with speaking in

tongues, as a reality in their lives.[5]

THE ROLE OF THE HOLY SPIRIT IN INSPIRING OUR WORSHIP

We have discussed how God demands that we worship Him in Spirit and in truth. We have talked briefly about how important it is that we allow the Holy Spirit to inspire our worship. We will now discuss how the Spirit of God helps in inspiring worship.

How the Spirit Inspires Our Worship

The Spirit of God plays an important role in our worship of God. When we allow the Spirit to enter into our worship services, He inspires us and causes our hearts to be lifted up in

praise to God. There are at least three ways the Holy Spirit inspires our worship:

1. He brings us into a loving relationship with God. Paul wrote of how the Holy Spirit prompts true worship. He spoke of the "Spirit of adoption" (Rom. 8:15) who leads us into an intimate relationship with God. As the Spirit of God moves in our hearts, we are made to feel the love of God (5:5). This divine warming of our hearts causes us to cry out in worship, "Abba, Father" (8:15).

2. He lifts up Jesus. Not only does the Spirit bring us into a

---

[5] Bob Sorge, *Exploring Worship: A Practical Guide to Praise and Worship,* (New Wilmington, PA: Son-Rise Publications, 1987, 80.

loving relationship with God, He also lifts up Jesus in our midst. Jesus stated that, when the Spirit of Truth comes, "He will bring glory to me" (John 16:14). When the Holy Spirit fills our spirits, He reveals to us the Lordship of Christ. And by the Spirit we cry out, "Jesus is Lord!" (1 Cor. 12:3). Jesus is exalted in our hearts, and our mouths are filled with praise to Him.

3. He prompts us to worship. Throughout Scripture we see the Holy Spirit inspiring the people of God to worship. In the Old Testament, He inspired the prophetess, Miriam, the sister of Moses, to lead the women of Israel in worship (Exod. 15:20). The Spirit of God came powerfully on upon King Saul, causing him to join a band of prophets who were worshiping God with lyres, tambourines, flutes, and harps (1 Sam. 10:5-11). Saul was inspired by the Spirit to enter into their prophetic worship with them. It was the Spirit who inspired David and the other Psalmists to pen the Psalms, the praise book of Israel.

We also see the Holy Spirit inspiring and prompting worship in the New Testament church. On the Day of Pentecost those who were filled with the Spirit were heard "declaring the wonders of God" in the languages of the nations (Acts 2:11). At the house of Cornelius, those who received the Holy Spirit spoke with tongues and magnified God (Acts 10:46). The Spirit inspired the church in Corinth to worship God (1 Cor. 14:16-17, 25-26), and He inspired the Philippian church to do the same (Phil. 3:3). The same is true today. Those who have learned to depend upon the Spirit of the Lord have discovered a glorious freedom in expressing their worship to God, for "where the Spirit of the Lord is there is freedom" (2 Cor. 3:17).

The Importance of Personal Preparation

If the Spirit of the Lord is such a wonderful ally in our worship, does it not follow that we should all be filled with the Spirit? If we truly want to worship God as He desires, we should let His Spirit fill us to overflowing. Paul told the Ephesians to "be filled with the Spirit" (Eph. 5:18). This filling in the Spirit would result in Spirit-inspired songs of praise and thanksgiving (vv. 19-20). Sorge wrote,

> Spiritual worship is the exclusive privilege of those who have been quickened by the indwelling Holy Spirit . . . The Holy Spirit is an integral part of our worship, and congregational worship is successful only as we submit to him as our divine Worship Leader.[6]

We must be full of the Spirit of the Lord if we are to truly worship God in Spirit and in truth. Each believer should prepare his or her own heart before the public worship service (1 Cor. 14:26). This personal preparation should include prayer and meditation of the Word of God. It should also include a fresh infilling with the Holy Spirit. Only then will we be ready to enter in to true worship in Spirit and in truth.

THE ROLE OF THE HOLY SPIRIT IN DIRECTING WORSHIP

Having talked about the role of the Spirit in inspiring our worship, we now turn to the role of the Holy Spirit in directing our worship.

---

[6] Ibid, 77.

The True Worship Leader

If a people are to genuinely worship in the Spirit, they must see the Holy Spirit as their true Worship Leader. Every action must be taken in submission to, and under the direction of, the Spirit of God. It is in this context that Paul instructs the Corinthian church concerning the operation of spiritual gifts in their worship services.[7] He told them that in these congregational gatherings the Holy Spirit would distribute gifts—or "manifestations"—of the Spirit (12:7). He would do this "to each one, just as he determines" (v. 11). Through the revelation gifts, He would give insight and direction. Through the prophetic gifts, He would speak words of "strengthening, encouragement and comfort" (14:3), and through the power gifts, He would perform His mighty works in their midst. The Holy Spirit was to be their true Worship Leader.

In the book of Acts we are given an example of the Holy Spirit directing a worship service. This took place in the church at Antioch:

> While they were worshiping the Lord and fasting, the Holy Spirit said, "Set apart for me Barnabas and Saul for the work to which I have called them." So after they had fasted and prayed, they placed their hands on them and sent them off. (13:1-3)

The Holy Spirit Himself was serving as the church's Worship Leader. It was He who set the tone for the service, and it was He

---

[7] In this section of the book of 1 Corinthians Paul was talking about when believers "came together" for public worship (1 Cor. 11:17-20, 33, 34; 14:23, 26).

who gave them directions as to how to proceed. The same order should mark our worship services today. If we are to truly worship in the Spirit, we should look to the Spirit of God as our Worship Leader.

Following the Leader

While the Holy Spirit should be the true Worship Leader in our worship services, it is nonetheless apparent that each service will also need a person to chair and to lead that service. If the congregation is be lead into true worship in the Spirit, it is essential that that person know how to follow the leading of the Holy Spirit. He or she must be very sensitive to the Holy Spirit and must never wrest the service out of His hands. The worship leader must at all times remain open and sensitive to the promptings of the Holy Spirit. He must be prepared to flow with the Spirit. Sorge spoke about this responsibility of the worship leader:

> Many worship leaders are frustrated because they have not learned to follow the Holy Spirit's guidance in the context of a worship service. God wants to do specific things in each worship service, and unless we move with Him, we can miss His purpose.

It becomes vital, then, that we be sensitive to the gentle promptings of the Spirit as the service is in progress.[8]

It is also necessary that the pastor takes time to teach his

---

[8] Sorge, 77.

congregation how to follow and respond to the leadership of the Spirit.

What can be done to ensure that the Spirit of the Lord is present in our worship services? How should we respond to His presence? How can we follow His lead? There are two areas to which we must give particular attention if we are to truly worship God in the Spirit:

1. Appropriating the Spirit's presence. If the Spirit is to come and direct our congregational worship, we must begin our worship by taking the necessary steps to ensure that He is present. We must prayerfully and purposefully set the stage for His coming. We do this in two ways:

Prayer. First, we can appropriate the Spirit's presence in our services by prayer. This prayer should take place both before and during the worship service. Before our worship services we should spend time in prayer, preparing our hearts for the coming worship experience. During this time of prayer we should make a conscious effort to submit our wills to the will of the Holy Spirit. We should seek direction from Him for this particular service. We should pray, "Holy Spirit, what is Your will for the service? What do You want to accomplish?" If necessary, we should repent of any sins or carnal attitudes that might hinder the Spirit's moving.

Such spiritual preparation is especially important for every person who will assume any leadership role in the service (cf. 1 Cor 14:26). It is important that the pastor, the chairman, the song leader, the worship team, the special singers, the musicians, and anyone else who will participate in the service come early for a time of prayer and seeking God for His direction. Each one should also ask God for a fresh infilling of His Spirit.

Prayer should also be offered during the worship service. At the beginning of the service it is good to lead the congregation in a prayer inviting the Holy Spirit to come and have His way in the service. We can pray, "Come, Holy Spirit." Then, we can open our minds and our spirits to receive Him. As a result of such prayer, we can legitimately expect the Holy Spirit to come and manifest His presence in our midst (Matt. 18:19-20).

Praise. A second way we can appropriate the presence of the Holy Spirit into our worship services is through congregational praise. Praise and adoration help prepare the way for the manifestation of God's Spirit. The Bible says that God dwells in the praises of His people (Ps. 22:2, KJV). As Paul and Silas prayed and sang hymns to God in a Roman jail, the Holy Spirit manifested His presence: "Suddenly there was such a violent earthquake that the foundations of the prison were shaken. At once all the prison doors flew open, and everybody's chains came loose" (Acts 16: 26). We too, as we sing and shout our praises to God, can expect the Holy Spirit to come and manifest His presence in our midst.

2. Responding to the Spirit's presence. A second area to which we must give our attention, if we are to truly worship God in the Spirit, is the area of responding to the Spirit's presence. Once the Spirit comes, it is essential that we properly respond to Him. We can respond to the Spirit's presence in three very practical ways:

By acknowledging His presence. Our first response to the Spirit's presence could be to simply acknowledge His presence. Just as we would never be guilty of ignoring a guest who came into our home, we should never be guilty of ignoring our Remarkable Friend when He comes into our worship services. At church we take time to recognize visitors and properly greet those who come into our services. We should also take time to acknowledge the presence of our heavenly Visitor. We should pray, "Holy Spirit, You are *indeed* welcome in this place. Take Your place of honor in our worship service. Be enthroned in our praises!" (cf. Ps. 21:2).

By submitting to His will. A second way we can respond to the presence of the Spirit in our church services is by submitting to His will. We should remember that He is sovereign, that He has a will for every church service, and that He comes to fulfill that will. We must be ready to submit our wills to His. At times, He will reveal His will to us in our prayer time before the service. On other occasions, He reveals His will to us "en route," that is, as the worship service proceeds. We should be constantly vigilant and open to His leading.

Throughout the service the worship leader and the pastor must constantly pray, "Lord, what is your will for this service? What are You wanting to accomplish? What can we do now to see that Your will is done?"

By releasing spiritual gifts. A final way that believers can respond to the presence of the Holy Spirit in their worship services is by being prepared to release spiritual gifts as the Spirit directs and prompts. He will want to work through the Spirit-filled members of the congregation to manifest His presence. He has come to give direction through words of knowledge or wisdom. He has come to speak words of encouragement and edification to the congregation. And He has come to heal the sick and destroy the works of Satan. These things will happen only as God's people respond to Him and in faith allow Him to use them in the manifestation of spiritual gifts.

One important role of the Holy Spirit in the lives of Spirit-filled believers is inspiring and directing them in their worship of God. We must know that it is only with the help of the Spirit of God that we can truly worship God. We must remain ever open to His leadership in this area.

CHAPTER 13

MINISTRY

IN THE SPIRIT

Someone has rightly observed that a person can do the work of God in one of two ways. He can do in his own strength, or he can do it in God's strength. It has been my sad observation that most Christians have chosen the first way rather than the second. I once read where someone said if God were to withdraw His Spirit from most Pentecostal churches today, ninety-five percent of what is being done in those churches would continue unaffected. This is tragic, since Jesus has promised the church divine power to do the work of God.

In this chapter, and the two that follow, we will look into how the Holy Spirit empowers us for ministry. We will talk about how the Christian worker can appropriate and exercise that power. But first, let's look more closely at how the Holy Spirit equips us for ministry.

THE HOLY SPIRIT EQUIPS US FOR EFFECTIVE MINISTRY

Charismatic theologian J. Rodman Williams describes the Holy Spirit as the "Enabling Spirit."[1] It is He who enables us to do effective ministry by equipping and empowering us to do the will of God.

Power to Get the Job Done

The Holy Spirit gives to us the necessary power to accomplish our God-given mandate. Jesus concluded His earthly ministry by issuing two commands to His emerging church. First, He commanded them to preach the gospel to all nations (Matt. 28:18-20; Mark 16:16-18; Luke 24:47-48; John 20:21). Today, we call this command the Great Commission. Fulfilling this commission is the church's primary reason for being. Secondly, Jesus commanded His church to wait until they were empowered by the Holy Spirit (Luke 24:49; Acts 1:4-8). Before it can fulfill Jesus' first command, the church must obey His second.

In Acts 1:8 Jesus gave a promise: "You will receive power when the Holy Spirit comes on you, and you will be my witnesses in Jerusalem, and in all Judea and Samaria, and to the ends of the earth." The disciples received this power when they were baptized in the Holy Spirit on the Day of Pentecost (Acts 2:4). Today, the baptism in the Holy Spirit continues to be an indispensable part of any Christian worker's equipment.

---

[1] Rodman Williams, *Renewal Theology*, II (Grand Rapids: Zondervan Publishing House, 1988), 155.

In Chapter 3 we discussed the many wonderful blessings that come into one's life by being baptized in the Holy Spirit. Personal blessing, however, is not the primary purpose of Spirit baptism. The primary purpose of the baptism in the Holy Spirit is empowerment for missional witness (Acts 1:8). Through the baptism in the Holy Spirit the Christian worker is empowered and equipped for effective service. This equipping for service includes powerful gifts of the Holy Spirit (1 Cor. 12:7-11). Thus equipped, the minister has the power he or she needs to get the job done.

The Examples of Jesus and the New Testament Church

We can more clearly see how the Holy Spirit equips us for effective service by looking briefly at the examples of Jesus and the New Testament believers.

The example of Jesus. Jesus came to earth to give His life as a ransom for all people (Matt. 20:28, 1 Tim. 2:6). He also came to be an example to us as to how we should live and minister (John 13:15, 1 Pet. 2:21). He set down the pattern for ministry that we should follow. But how did He minister? The Bible teaches that He ministered in the power and anointing of the Holy Spirit: "How God anointed Jesus of Nazareth with the Holy Spirit and power, and how he went around doing good and healing all who were under the power of the devil, because God was with him (Acts 10:38).

Jesus was first anointed by the Spirit at his baptism (Luke 3:21-22). He then went out and ministered in the Spirit's power (4:1, 14, 18-19; 5:17). In doing this, Jesus set the pattern of ministry for those of us who would follow Him until the end of the age (Matt. 28:20). Now, we must follow His example. We, like Him, must first be empowered by the Holy Spirit, then, and only then, can we go out and minister in power.

The example of the New Testament church. Like Jesus, the primitive church ministered in the power and anointing of the Holy Spirit. The church was first empowered on the Day of Pentecost (Acts 2:4). As a result of this divine infusion of power, the first disciples went out and ministered in power, and with great effectiveness. They were simply following the pattern set down by Jesus—first be empowered, then minister.

As did Jesus and the apostolic church, we too must minister in the power and anointing of the Holy Spirit. How foolish we would be to think that we can minister without His enabling presence. We must never attempt ministry without first having been filled with the Holy Spirit.

THE HOLY SPIRIT ENABLES US IN OUR MINISTRY

Not only does the Holy Spirit give us the power necessary to do ministry, He also enables us in the performance of our ministries. He helps us day by day to discharge our God-given duties. There are many ways he does this. Let's examine five:

He Inspires Us To Do Ministry

It is the Holy Spirit who calls and inspires us in ministry. When Peter was asked why he went to Caesarea to preach to the Gentiles there, he replied, "The Spirit told me to have no hesitation about going" (Acts 11:12). The Holy Spirit inspired

him to go in faith. Today, the Spirit will also inspire us to do ministry in the following ways:

1. A burden for the lost. First, the Holy Spirit will give to us a burden for the lost. He does this by opening our eyes and our hearts to the many lost people all around us. Too often, like the blind man of Bethsaida, we see people as if they were only "trees walking around" (Mark 8:24). Tragically, we have little concern for the many lost people we meet every day. However, if we will allow Him, the Holy Spirit will change our hearts. He will move us with compassion for the lost.

Several times in the gospels we read of Jesus being moved with compassion over the needs of people (Matt. 14:14; Mark 1:41, 6:34). In a similar way, the Holy Spirit will inspire us to do ministry by giving us a burden for the many lost people in our communities.

2. A love for the church. Not only will the Holy Spirit create in our hearts a burden for the lost, He will also give to us a love for other Christians—that same love that Jesus Himself has (Eph. 5:25). Out of this sincere love for our brothers and sisters in Christ, we will be motivated to become effective pastors and Christian workers.

3. A vision for world harvest. In addition to giving to us a burden for the lost and a love for the church, the Holy Spirit will give to us a vision for world harvest. He will open our eyes to a perishing world that desperately needs to hear the message of Christ.

One time when Jesus saw the multitudes, He was moved with compassion because "they were harassed and helpless, like sheep without a shepherd." Then He said, "The harvest is plentiful but the workers are few. Ask the Lord of the harvest, therefore, to send out laborers into his harvest field" (Matt. 9:37,

38).

Jesus is the Lord of the Harvest, and yet, we know that when He returned to the Father, He handed over His work on earth to the Holy Spirit (John 15:26, 16:6-11). As a result, the Spirit is now overseeing the harvest. We could therefore say that the Holy Spirit is the Superintendent of the Harvest. When we pray to the Lord of the Harvest, He will send the Superintendent of the Harvest to give us a vision for world harvest. In the book of Acts the Holy Spirit directed the church into missions involvement (Acts 10:19; 13:1-4; 16:6-10). Today, if we will submit ourselves to Him, He will also give us a vision for world evangelism.

He Empowers our Witness to the Lost

A second way that the Holy Spirit enables us in ministry is by empowering us to witness to the lost. Jesus promised, "You will receive power when the Holy Spirit comes on you; and you will be my witnesses" (Acts 1:8). As a result of being filled with the Spirit, we will be emboldened to witness for Christ.

In the book of Acts, what was once a frightened group of disillusioned disciples became a mighty evangelistic force. As a result of their Spirit-anointed witness, thousands were brought into kingdom of God. We too can become powerful witnesses for Christ if we will allow the Holy Spirit to fill us and use us in His harvest field. This empowering to witness includes at least three dimensions:

1. Divine insight. As we witness for Christ, the Holy Spirit will give us divine insight into the Scriptures to aid us in effectively explaining them to the lost. This very thing happened in the ministry of Philip when he witnessed to the Ethiopian on the Gaza road (Acts 8:29-34). The Holy Spirit gave Philip supernatural insight into the Scriptures. As a result, Philip was able to persuasively preach Christ to the African traveler.

We can expect the Holy Spirit to do the same for us today. If we will appropriate His presence, He will give us His insight into the situation; He will bring key passages of Scripture to mind as we need them; and He will give us the wisdom we need to know how to apply these Scriptures to the lives of those to whom we are witnessing (Prov. 11:30; 1 Cor. 12:8).

2. Anointed words. Not only will the Holy Spirit empower our witness to the lost by giving us insight into the Scriptures, He will also anoint the words we speak to them. This supernatural touch on our words will give them greater persuasive power. As Stephen spoke, those who listened to him "could not stand up against his wisdom or the Spirit by whom he spoke" (Acts 6:10). In the same way, if we will yield ourselves to the Holy Spirit, He will anoint our words and give them persuasive power.

3. Gifts of the Holy Spirit. Another way the Holy Spirit will give persuasive power to our witness is through the gifts of the Holy Spirit (1 Cor. 12:7-11). Through the manifestation of the power gifts (the gift of faith, gifts of healing, and miraculous powers) He will supernaturally confirm the gospel we preach. Through the revelation gifts (word of knowledge, word of wisdom, and discerning of spirits) He will give us supernatural insight into the individual needs of the people to whom we are witnessing. He will also give us wisdom as to how to proceed with our witness. And through prophetic gifts (prophecy, the gift of tongues, and the interpretation of tongues) He will give us the words we need to convince the lost that they should call on

Christ.

He Anoints Our Preaching and Teaching

A third way the Holy Spirit enables ministry is by anointing our preaching and teaching. As Peter preached under a powerful anointing of the Holy Spirit, his listeners "were cut to the heart and said to Peter and the other apostles, 'Brothers, what shall we do?'" (Acts 2:37). In the same way, the Spirit anointed other early believers as they preached the Word. When we speak of the anointing, we speak of the manifest presence of God that comes upon a Spirit-filled individual who is involved in ministry. This presence enables him to minister with greater effectiveness and power than he would have been able to in his own strength and ability. This supernatural anointing is an absolute necessity for effective gospel ministry.

While some see the importance of the anointing of the Holy Spirit in a preaching ministry, they see little connection between the anointing and teaching. And yet, the anointing of the Holy Spirit plays a major role in the New Testament model for teaching.

Concerning Jesus' teaching ministry the Bible says, "Jesus returned to Galilee in the power of the Spirit . . . [and] He taught in their synagogues" (Luke 4:14-5). On another occasion "as he [Jesus] was teaching, . . . the power of the Lord was present for him to heal the sick" (Luke 5:17). Notice how, as Jesus taught the people, the Holy Spirit was powerfully present. In like manner, we should expect the Holy Spirit to be present in our teaching ministries.

If we will prepare ourselves and yield ourselves to Him, the Holy Spirit will anoint our preaching and teaching just as He did the preaching and teaching ministries of Jesus and the apostles.

He Verifies the Word

A fourth way that the Holy Spirit will enable us in ministry is that He will verify the word that we preach through demonstrations of supernatural power. After Pentecost there was a dramatic release of miracle-working power in the disciples' ministries. This release of divine power resulted in, among other things,

- speaking in tongues (2:4)
- anointed preaching (2:14ff, 4:31, 6:10, 8:25)
- powerful healings (3:1-8; 5:15; 6:7)
- signs and wonders (2:43, 5:12, 6:8, 8:6)
- powerful manifestations of God's presence (4:31)
- demonic deliverances (5:16, 6:7)
- supernatural deliverance from danger (5:19)
- visions (6:55-56)
- Holy Spirit baptisms (2:4, 8:17).

All of this was in accordance with the promise of Jesus. He had promised them that, as they went into the world to preach the gospel, supernatural signs would follow their preaching:

> And these signs will accompany those who believe: In my name they will drive out demons; they will pick up snakes with their hands; and when they drink deadly poison, it will not hurt them at all; they will place their hands on sick people, and they will get well. (Mark 16:17-18)

Even today, if we will go out and preach the gospel in the

power of the Holy Spirit, we can expect the same supernatural results. We can expect God to confirm His Word with signs following.[2]

He Enables Us to Live a Christ-like Lifestyle

A final way that the Holy Spirit enables the Christian worker in ministry is by imparting to him or her a Christ-like lifestyle. Donald Gee wrote, "Jesus Christ is the greatest example of the principle that spiritual power is found where supernatural gifts and spotless holiness exist in perfect balance."[3]

Jesus' power to move people came not only from His miraculous works, but also from His beautiful life. Christ's life was characterized by purity and gracious speech, as well as by powerful signs. Together these elements had a powerful effect on those to whom He ministered. The people wondered at his purity (Mark 7:37), they were amazed at his gracious words (Luke 4:22), and they flocked to see and experience His powerful works (Matt. 4:23-25).

We too must allow the Holy Spirit to work in our lives, producing in us a Christ-like lifestyle. Like His beautiful life, our lives must be characterized by grace and purity.

---

[2] We will expand on this discussion in more detail Chapter 15.

[3] David Womack, ed., *Pentecostal Experience, The Writings of Donald Gee, Settling the Question of Doctrine versus Experience* (Springfield, MO: Gospel Publishing House, 1993), 98-99.

HOW TO ENSURE THE SPIRIT'S HELP IN MINISTRY

If we will properly prepare ourselves, we can be assured that the Holy Spirit will equip and enable us in our ministries. To do this we must do at least three things:

Be Filled with the Spirit

As we have mentioned in almost every chapter of this book, a primary requirement for Christian life and ministry in the Spirit is the baptism in the Holy Spirit. No one should ever attempt to minister for Christ without this powerful enabling experience.

Walk in the Spirit

A second thing one must do to ensure the Spirit's enablement in ministry is to learn to daily walk in the Spirit. Walking in the Spirit goes beyond one's initial baptism in the Spirit. It can only be accomplished through a life of holiness, prayer, and yieldedness to the Spirit. Walking in the Spirit also requires periodic refillings with the Spirit.[4]

As we walk in the Spirit, we must learn to respond to the Spirit's directives. Jesus ministered through the power of the Spirit, but He also followed the Spirit's guidance. The same can be said of Peter, of Paul, and of others in the New Testament church. And the same must be said of us today, if we are to truly minister in the Spirit's power.

---

[4] For a more complete teaching on walking in the Spirit please review Chapter 10.

Obedience and Faith

A final way we can ensure the Spirit's aid in our ministries is by appropriating the Spirit's help through obedience and faith. When one has been filled with the Spirit, and has learned how to live his life under the Spirit's guidance, he can expect many ministry opportunities to come his way. These opportunities will often come unexpectedly as he goes about his daily duties. They will include opportunities to witness, opportunities to give godly counsel, and opportunities to intervene in personal crises. These personal crises will often involve interpersonal conflicts, sickness, or demon possession. At such times, the Holy Spirit will direct the Spirit-filled minister concerning how to properly respond.

Once the Christian worker listens for and hears the voice of the Spirit, he or she must then appropriate the Spirit's help through acts of obedience and faith. These two elements, obedience and faith, are key in releasing the power of the Spirit into a ministry situation. Let's look briefly at each of these elements:

1. Obedience. The Spirit of God comes to anoint us only as we act in obedience to the Word of God and to His inner promptings. Let me illustrate what I mean. As we learned in Chapter 10, the Spirit stands ready to come and illuminate the Scriptures and help us to understand them. However, before He can illuminate the Scriptures to us, there must be an act of obedience on our part. We must first obey the Word, and take the initiative and begin reading the Scriptures (2 Tim. 2:15).

It is at this point—the point of obedience—that the Spirit comes to anoint us. How can He help us to understand the Bible, if we don't take the initiative, pick it up, and begin to read it? But once we act in obedience, and begin to prayerfully read the Word, the anointing comes to aid us in our understanding.

The same can be said about prayer. In Chapter 11 we learned how the Spirit of God stands ready to help us in prayer. But if we never act in obedience to God and begin to pray, how can the Spirit come and help us? If, however, we will obey and begin to pray, the anointing will come (Rom. 8:26-27).

Now lets apply this principle to witnessing. The Spirit is prepared to anoint us and help us witness for Christ (Acts 1:8). However, before He will come to us and anoint our witness, we must first, in obedience to God's Word, take the initiative and begin witnessing to someone. When we do, the Spirit of God will come to anoint, inspire, and enable us.

Many modern Christians have been filled with the Spirit, and yet they have failed to become effective witnesses for Christ. Why is this? It is because they refuse to obey God, and witness to those with whom they come into contact. They seem to be waiting on the Spirit to coerce them into witnessing. He will never do this. However, if we will take the initiative, He will come to our aid, anoint us, and empower our witness for

Christ. The principle is this: we must first obey, then the Spirit will come to anoint and enable us.

2. Faith. Faith is another essential element in appropriating the Spirit's help in ministry. It is, therefore, very important, when opportunities to minister come, that the Spirit-filled minister know how to act in faith. As we have stated above, when we obey the voice of the Spirit the anointing comes. However, once the anointing has come, it must then be released by an act of faith. Remember this, the anointing comes as a result of an act of obedience, but the anointing is released as a result of an act of faith.

Faith is like an electrical switch. A flip of the switch releases the potential electrical power waiting in the electrical lines. Although the power is there, it is not released to do its work until the switch is flipped. In the same way, the anointing to preach, prophesy, or heal the sick is released by an act of faith on the part of the Spirit-filled believer.

This is how it works: A ministry opportunity presents itself. The Spirit-filled believer discerns the Spirit's voice prompting him to minister in the situation. He now has a choice to make. He can obey the Spirit's voice, or he can ignore it. If he obeys, the anointing will come; if he disobeys the anointing will subside. Once the minister obeys the Spirit's voice and begins to minister, he must now begin to act and minister boldly in the realm of faith. It will be through faith that the anointing will be released into the life of the needy individual and the need will be met.

Jesus has commanded us to preach the gospel to the nations. He has instructed us to minister in the same power and anointing in which He ministered. We can do this only through the enablement of the Holy Spirit.

CHAPTER 14

GIFTS AND FRUIT

OF THE SPIRIT

It is often debated among believers which is the most needed in the Christian life—the gifts of the Spirit or the fruit of the Spirit. But it is a pointless argument. The obvious answer is that both are necessary. Authentic Christian witness involves both manifesting spiritual gifts and exhibiting spiritual fruit. As the gifts and fruit of the Spirit appear together in the Christian's life, his or her witness to the world becomes greater. At the same time the believer's benefit to the church increases. In this chapter we will look at two related issues concerning the gifts and fruit of the Spirit in the Christian's life. First, we will discuss how spiritual gifts and spiritual fruit relate to one another. Then, we will look at how they operate in the Christian life.

GIFTS AND FRUIT COMPARED
AND CONTRASTED

We will begin this chapter by identifying and defining the gifts and fruit of the Spirit. We will then compare and contrast spiritual gifts and spiritual fruit as to their origins and their proposes.

Gifts of the Spirit

In the writings of Paul there are three main listings of spiritual gifts: one in Romans 12, another in Ephesian 4, and another in 1 Corinthians 12. Bible scholars have pointed out that a close examination of the contexts of these listings of spiritual gifts reveals the cooperative work of each member of the Trinity in dispensing them, as follows:

- *Gifts of the Father* (Rom. 12:6-8). In Romans 12:3 Paul states that "God has given" each of these gifts to members of the body of Christ. These gifts could thus be properly called "Gifts of the Father."
- *Gifts of Christ* (Eph. 4:11). Ephesians 4:7 states that these gifts are given "as Christ apportioned." Because of this, they are sometimes referred to as the "Ministry Gifts of Christ."
- *Gifts of the Holy Spirit* (1 Cor. 12:8-10). In 1 Corinthians 12:7 Pall calls this listing of gifts "the manifestation of the Spirit." Also, note the repeated phrases "by the Spirit" (vv. 3, 9), "through the Spirit" (v. 8), and "by means of . . . the Spirit (v. 8). These gifts alone can be accurately called "Gifts of the Spirit."

In this chapter we will focus our attention on the nine gifts of the Holy Spirit as listed in 1 Corinthians 12:8-10. Concerning these gifts Rodman Williams affirms, "Let it be firmly said that the church cannot be fully or freely the church without the presence and operation of the gifts of the Holy Spirit. What is depicted therefore in 1 Corinthians—and recurring in our day—is in no sense a peripheral matter but is crucial to the life of the church."[1]

These gifts represent the various ways in which the Spirit of God manifests His presence in the midst of His people. Paul's list reads like this:

> Now to each one the manifestation of the Spirit is given for the common good. To one there is given through the Spirit the message of wisdom, to another the message of knowledge by means of the same Spirit, to another faith by the same Spirit, to another gifts of healing by that one Spirit, to another miraculous powers, to another prophecy, to another distinguishing between spirits, to another speaking in different kinds of tongues, and to still another the interpretation of tongues. (1 Cor. 12:7-10)

These nine gifts of the Spirit can be defined as *supernatural anointings given by the Spirit of God through Spirit-filled believers to accomplish the will of the Father.* They are manifested in the believer according to the will of the Spirit (1 Cor. 12:11). They come as anointings, or movings, of the Holy Spirit upon the yielded believer. And they are released as the believer responds and acts in faith.

These spiritual gifts are often placed into three categories to aid in our understanding them. Those categories, along with a definition of each gift, are as follows:

1. Revelation Gifts: (Given to know the mind of God).

---

[1] Ibid, p. 327.

- *Word (message) of knowledge:* A Spirit-conferred revelation of a portion of God's knowledge.
- *Word (message) of wisdom:* A Spirit-conferred revelation of a portion of God's wisdom.
- *Distinguishing between spirits:* A Spirit-conferred revelation of what S[s]pirit is being manifested or motivating an action.

2. *Power Gifts:* (Given to do the works of God).

- *Faith:* A Spirit-energized surge of faith to accomplish a God-ordained task.
- *Gifts of healing:* A Spirit-energized healing of diseases and infirmities.
- *Miraculous powers:* A Spirit-energized release of divine power to accomplish a special work of God.

3. *Prophetic Gifts* (Given to speak the words of God).

- *Prophecy:* A Spirit-inspired speaking forth of a message from God.
- *Tongues:* A Spirit-inspired speaking forth of a message from God, or a prayer to God, in a language not known to the speaker.
- *Interpretation of Tongues:* A Spirit-inspired speaking forth of the meaning of a message or prayer spoken in tongues.

It is expected that every Spirit-filled believer will be used in the operation of spiritual gifts in accordance with the will of the Spirit (1 Cor. 12:7, 11; 14:26). We should covet these gifts

and anticipate being used by God to release them in ministry (1 Cor. 14:1, 39).

Fruit of the Spirit

Not only does Paul speak of nine gifts of the Holy Spirit, he also speaks of nine "fruit of the Spirit": "But the fruit of the Spirit is love, joy, peace, patience, kindness, goodness, faithfulness, gentleness and self control. Against such things there is no law" (Gal. 5:22-23). These fruit of the Spirit can be defined as *Christ-like qualities of character that are produced in believers lives as they live their lives under the Spirit's influence.* They are Christian graces that have to do with godly attitudes, character, and life-style.

Paul contrasts the fruit of the Spirit (Gal. 5:22-23) with the works of the flesh (5:19-21). The one is the opposite of the other. The fruit of the Spirit spring supernaturally from a life yielded to the Spirit of God. The works of the flesh arise naturally out of a life yielded to the carnal nature.

It is important that we not confuse these spiritual fruit with mere human qualities that are produced as a result of human effort and refinement. We could call these character qualities "natural" fruit. Natural fruit originates in the heart of man and is attained by natural means. Spiritual fruit, however, has its origin in the character of Christ, and are attained through the work of the Holy Spirit in the human life.

Compared and Contrasted as to Origin and Purpose

In order that we might better understand the gifts and fruit

of the Spirit it helps to compare and contrast them as to their origins and their purposes.

Origin. Spiritual gifts and spiritual fruit have a common origin. Both have their origin in the Spirit of God. Neither originate in human ability, intelligence or effort.

Purpose. Just as they have a common origin, spiritual gifts and spiritual fruit also have a common two-fold purpose. They both serve to build up the body of Christ and to advance the kingdom of God in the earth. They accomplish this, however, in different ways. The manifestation of spiritual gifts helps to edify the body of Christ through demonstrations of God's power and presence in the church. In the same way they help to fulfill the task of world evangelization.

Spiritual fruit build up the body of Christ in a different way. As believers grow in the grace and knowledge of Christ (2 Pet. 3:18), Christ's character is reproduced in their lives. As love, joy, peace, patience, and the other fruit of the Spirit come into believers' lives, the church grows strong. As people on the outside see these qualities in the Christian community, they are attracted to Christ and the kingdom of God grows.

Compared and Contrasted as to How Each is Acquired

Although both the gifts of the Spirit and the fruit of the Spirit have their origin in the Spirit of God, and although they both serve to build up the body of Christ and to advance the kingdom of God in the earth, they are acquired by different means. Let's look briefly at how each is acquired.

Gifts of the Spirit. These manifestations of the Spirit are given as free gifts of God's grace. They require no effort or achievement on the part of the recipient. They are freely given to Spirit-filled believers based on no personal merit, and they are distributed according to the sovereign will of the Holy Spirit. Once the gift is given, the Spirit-filled believer needs only to act in faith in order that the gift might be released, and thus accomplish its intended purpose.

Fruit of the Spirit. Like spiritual gifts, spiritual fruit are acquired by faith. Unlike spiritual gifts, however, spiritual fruit must be cultivated and grow in the Christian life. They are not manifested in full at the moment of faith, as are spiritual gifts, but grow gradually in the believer's life as a result of his daily submitting to the Spirit (Gal. 5:16-25) and abiding in Christ (John 15:1-8).

Compared and Contrasted as to Their Meaning

What does it tell us about a person's spiritual life when he or she is often used in manifesting spiritual gifts? What does it say about them when their lives are characterized by the fruit of the Spirit?

Manifesting Spiritual Gifts. When God uses an individual in manifesting a spiritual gift, it tells us something about God, and it also tells us something about that person.

- *About God.* What does the manifestation of spiritual gifts tell us about God? Two things: First, it tells us that God is gracious and He wants to use and bless His children. Further, it tells us that God loves His church and desires to see it built up and strengthened.

- *About the one being used.* When God uses a person in manifesting spiritual gifts, it also tells us something about that person manifesting the gift. It tells us that that person has been filled with the Spirit, and that he or she is a yielded vessel, open to the working of the Spirit of God in his or her own spirit.

• *What it does not tell us.* It is important to understand what being used to minister spiritual gifts does not indicate. It does not indicate that the person being used is necessarily spiritually mature, for God often uses even new Christians in the manifestation of spiritual gifts. Further, being used in a spiritual gift does not indicate that one is a truly spiritual person. God uses both the spiritually mature as well as the spiritually immature. (We will discuss this more in the next section.) Finally, being used in spiritual gifts does not indicate God's blanket approval on every aspect of that person's life.

Exhibiting Spiritual Fruit. What does the presence of spiritual fruit indicate about a person? Their presence in a person's life indicates at least two things:

• *Spiritual maturity.* When the fruit of the Spirit is evident in a believer's life, it indicates that that person is attaining to maturity in Christ. We can define Christian maturity as the quality of having the character and attitudes of Christ. Paul told the Philippian believers, "Your attitude should be the same as that of Christ Jesus" (Phil. 2:5). The nine fruit of the Spirit listed in Galatians 5:22-23 are a perfect description of the attitudes of Christ. When these attitudes are present in a believer, we can say that he or she is a mature Christian.

• *True spirituality.* The presence of spiritual fruit in a believers life also indicates true spirituality. The person who has these qualities can truly be described as a spiritual person.

In Galatians 6:1 Paul addressed his comments to "you who are spiritual." Who are these spiritual people to whom was Paul speaking? The answer is found in the preceding verses, Galatians 5:22-26. The person who is truly spiritual is the one who has "crucified the sinful nature with its passions and desires" (v. 24), is walking "in step with the Spirit" (v. 25), and is displaying the fruit of the Spirit in his or her life (vv. 22-23).

MANIFESTING GIFTS AND CULTIVATING FRUIT

Let's now discuss how spiritual gifts are manifested and how spiritual fruit is cultivated in the Christian life. First, we will discuss why both are needed.

Why Both Are Needed

Both spiritual gifts and spiritual fruit are needed for two reasons:

1. A total witness of the gospel. Both are needed in order that the church might present a total witness of the gospel to the outside world. Paul described how he went about preaching the gospel to the Gentiles. He said, "I have preached the full Gospel of Christ all the way from Jerusalem clear over to Illyricum" (Rom. 15:19, TLB). But, how did he present this "full Gospel"? He told us in the same verse: "I have won them by my message and by the good way I have lived before them, and by the miracles done through me as signs from God—all by the Holy Spirit's power" (v. 19, TLB).

We who call ourselves full-gospel Christians need to pay particular attention to these words of Paul. He is telling us how to preach the "full gospel of Christ." According to verse 19, for Paul it involved three things:

- *The message of Jesus Christ:* "I have won them by message . . ." (compare with Rom. 1:14-17).
- *The display of spiritual fruit:* " . . . and by the good way I have lived before them . . ."
- *The manifestation of spiritual gifts:* ". . . and by the miracles done through me as signs from God—all by the Holy Spirit's power."

As we go into the world to preach the gospel, we must be conscientious about giving a total witness of the gospel of Jesus Christ. This witness must include both a manifestation of spiritual gifts and a display of the spiritual fruit. Only then will our hearers be able to understand the true nature of the Christian faith.

2. The full image of Christ. A second reason why both spiritual gifts and spiritual fruit are needed is that believers must have both in their lives if they are to project the full image of Christ. People were attracted to Jesus for three reasons: because of His gracious words, because of His mighty works, and because of His beautiful life. Lets look briefly at each of these reasons:

His gracious words. Jesus testified, "The words that I have spoken to you are spirit and they are life" (John 6:63). His would-be captors said of Him, "No one ever spoke the way this man does" (7:46). As a result, the multitudes gathered to hear what He had to say. Luke says that "all spoke well of him and were amazed at the gracious words that came from his lips"

(Luke 4:22).

If we are going to present the full image of Christ to a dying world, we must do as Jesus did and preach the gospel under a sweet anointing of the Holy Spirit (Luke 4:18-19). As a result, gracious words will come from our lips as they did from His (4:22).

His mighty works. People were also attracted to Christ because of His mighty works. Matthew tells of Jesus performing many outstanding miracles. As a result "large crowds from Galilee, the Decapolis, Jerusalem, Judea and the region across the Jordan followed him" (4:25). On another day Jesus healed a man of leprosy. Because of this man's testimony, "Jesus could no longer enter a town openly but stayed outside in lonely places. Yet the people still came to him from everywhere" (Mark 1:45).

When we proclaim the gospel, we must present the full image of Christ to the people. We are not presenting the full image of Christ unless there is a demonstration of His power. When people see the power of God demonstrated through the operation of spiritual gifts, they will be attracted to Jesus and His life-changing message.

His beautiful life. People were also attracted to Christ because of His beautiful life. Pilate's testimony concerning Jesus was, "I find no fault in Him at all" (John 18:38, NKJV). The people of Decapolis declared, "He has done everything well (Mark 7:37).

Paul's listing of the nine fruit of the Spirit aptly describe the character of Jesus' life. His life was filled with love, joy, peace, patience, kindness, goodness, faithfulness, gentleness and self-control. These were His guiding principles. As a result, people were attracted to Him. Knowing that they would find an open heart and opened arms, the outcasts of society came unto Him. Beggars, lepers, publicans and sinners came. Even children were attracted to Him because of His beautiful life. If we are to present the full image of Jesus to those who need Him, our lives must the be imitations of His beautiful life. We must display the fruit of the Spirit in our lives and testimonies.

People will be attracted to us, and to Jesus in us, if our lives are examples of both His mighty works and His beautiful life. This can happen if we a manifesting both spiritual gifts and spiritual fruit.

Releasing Spiritual Gifts

Since spiritual gifts are so important in the life of the church and of Christians, the question naturally arises, What must one do to see spiritual gifts in operation in his or her life?

A thoughtful examination of the operation of spiritual gifts in the New Testament reveals that they are not received but released in the life of the Spirit-filled believer. The Bible speaks much about receiving the Holy Spirit (John 4:39; 14:17; 20:22; Acts 2:38; 8:15; 8:19; 2 Cor. 11:4; Gal. 3:14), but nowhere does it speak of receiving spiritual gifts. This is because, once a person has been baptized in the Holy Spirit, there is no longer any need to receive any spiritual gift. Since the gifts reside in the Spirit, and the Spirit resides in the Spirit-filled believer, it is logical to assume that all of the gifts reside in every Spirit-filled believer. They are released by the Spirit according to His sovereign will (1 Cor. 12:11) and the believer's eager desire (1 Cor. 12:31; 14:1, 39). They are simply manifestations of the Spirit of God who indwells and has empowered the Spirit-filled believer (1 Cor. 12:7).

When Paul speaks of spiritual gifts being "given" in 1 Corinthians 12-14, he does not mean that they are given out as personal possessions. They are rather given for the moment (i.e., "the manifestation of the Spirit is given" 12:7), and they are given in the context of a particular gathering of the church (11:17-18, 20, 33-34; 14:23, 26). Therefore, the phrase "to one is given" (12:7-8) is referring to a particular manifestation which occurs in a particular gathering of God's people. In that context, Paul says that not everyone will manifest a particular spiritual gift (12:30). But this does not mean that in the next gathering that any yielded, Spirit-filled believer cannot manifest any spiritual gift as the Spirit wills.

Neither does the Bible ever speak of discovering one's spiritual gift. One can hardly imagine the apostles sitting in a circle filling out personal profile charts in hopes of discovering their spiritual gifts. You may then ask, "Which gift do I have?" The answer is, if you are full of the Holy Spirit, you have all of the gifts. And if you will walk in the Spirit, the Spirit will use you in any way that He sees fit, releasing in you any gift that may be needed.

The question, then, is not, "How can I receive my spiritual gift?" or "How can I discover my spiritual gift?" The question that must be answered is "How can I live in such a way that the Spirit can manifest the spiritual gifts in my life as they are needed?"

Spiritual gifts are manifested as the result of the our responding in faith to an anointing of the Holy Spirit. When the Holy Spirit wants to manifest Himself in a particular spiritual gift, He will come as an anointing on a yielded believer. Once this anointing is sensed, it is then the duty of that believer to act in faith to release the spiritual gift. The act of faith could be to say or do a particular thing. This could be a humanly impossible act. Nevertheless, the believer must step out in faith. Once he takes such a step of faith, the anointing is released, the spiritual gift is manifested, and the work is accomplished.

Cultivating Spiritual Fruit

Spiritual fruit can only be cultivated by spiritual means. As we have already mentioned, it is important to realize that these fruit are not attained by natural means such as self-effort, positive thinking, or psychological "self-talk." Spiritual fruit must begin with spiritual experience. As one is born of the Spirit and filled with the Spirit, the seeds of spiritual fruit are planted in his or her life. The soil must then be cultivated in order for these seeds to grow and produce a harvest of spiritual fruit. These spiritual fruit can be cultivated in at least three ways:

1. By walking in the Spirit. As we walk in the Spirit, and live our lives under the Spirit's leadership and control (Gal. 5:16-18), spiritual fruit are produced and mature in our lives (vv. 22-23). Walking in the Spirit includes the following Christian disciplines:

- Crucifying the flesh with its passions and desires (Gal. 5:24).
- Setting ones mind on what the Spirit desires (Rom. 8:5).
- Being controlled by the Spirit (Rom. 8: 8).
- Putting to death the works of the flesh (Rom. 8:13).

- Being led by the Spirit (Rom.. 8:14).[2]

2. By abiding in Christ. A second way that one can cultivate spiritual fruit in his or her life is by abiding in Christ. Jesus taught that as we abide, or remain, in Him, spiritual fruit is produced in our lives (John 15:1-8). He described Himself as the main stem of the vine, and us as the branches. If a branch is severed from the vine, it will die, but if it abides in the vine, it will live and produce fruit. The same is true of us. If we remain in Christ, we will produce fruit. If we detach ourselves, we will die.

3. By attending to the means of grace. By means of grace we are speaking of those Christian practices which cause us to mature and grow in grace. They include the following:

- *Prayer and worship.* We should spend much time in private as well as corporate prayer and worship. These spiritual disciplines provide the proper spiritual climate for the growth of spiritual fruit in our lives.
- *Fellowship with other Christians.* The wise man said, "As iron sharpens iron, so one man sharpens another" (Pr. 27:17). As brothers and sisters in Christ spend time together, they sharpen one another through godly example and council. They encourage one another in the Christian life. As a result, spiritual fruit is fostered and cultivated in their lives.
- *Bible reading and meditation.* As the believer reads and

---

[2] For a more complete discussion on walking in the Spirit, see Chapter 7 of this book.

meditates on Scripture, his life is transformed and strengthened.

Both spiritual gifts and spiritual fruit are necessary qualities of the Christian life. If we as Christ's body are to fully represent Him to the world, we must possess both in abundance. As unbelievers see spiritual gifts in operation in the church, they are brought face to face with Christ's awesome power. As they see the fruit manifested in Christians, they are made to see His beautiful character. If the world is ever to truly see Christ in His church, we must earnestly covet both spiritual gifts and spiritual fruit in our lives and ministries.

Chapter 15

MINISTERING IN

SPIRITUAL POWER

Central to the worldview of the traditional African is the concept of power. It is the witch doctor's stock in trade. To the African, the word "medicine" translates "power." Medicine is the potion or charm that gives a man power over his adversary, or lover, or sickness, or you name it. Therefore, when ministering in the African context, the preacher who does not evidence spiritual power in his ministry has little impact on his audience. This is why it is so essential that anyone going to Africa to minister go in the power and anointing of the Holy Spirit.

The western church is fast learning that what is true for Africa is also true in the West. Postmodern man is looking for a religion of more than words and abstract concepts. He is looking for a religion that will address the pressing needs of his life, and that has the power to meet those needs. Sure, he is interested in issues of eternity, but his primary concern is the here and now. That is why any minister who expects to truly impact postmodern America must also be empowered by the Holy Spirit.

In this chapter we will discuss how the Holy Spirit helps us to minister with spiritual power. We will begin our discussion of power ministry with an extended definition. We will then talk about why power ministry is needed in the world today. And finally, we will offer some suggestions as to how one may actually do power ministry.[1]

POWER MINISTRY DEFINED

Let's begin our discussion of power ministry with a definition. Power ministry can be defined in three ways:

Ministry with a Powerful Plus

Power ministry is ministry with a powerful plus. By this we mean that it is a ministry with the added power of the Holy Spirit. Such a ministry has a tremendous advantage over a conventional ministry. When the power of the gospel (Rom. 1:15-16) is combined with the power of the Holy Spirit (Acts 1:8), there is created a tremendous force for advancing the kingdom of God.

Jesus Himself ministered in the power of the Holy Spirit (Acts 10:38). Mighty miracles and healings accompanied His teaching and preaching (Matt. 8:16, Luke 6:17-19). As a result, He preached and taught with great persuasive power (Luke 4:21; John 6:33, 7:46), and great crowds came to experience His ministry (Mark 1:45). The combination of these two factors, the power of the gospel and the power of the Holy Spirit, had a

---

[1] Many of the concepts presented in this chapter are taken from the author's book *Power Ministry: How to Minister in the Spirit's Power,* published by Africa's Hope, Springfield, MO, USA.

profound effect on those who heard and saw Him.

The early church also ministered with the powerful plus of the Spirit's power (Acts 4:33). This resulted in a mighty advance of the gospel, as recorded in the book of Acts. An oft-used term in the New Testament describing ministry in the supernatural is "signs and wonders" (Acts 2:29, 22, 43; 4:30; 5:12; 7:36; Rom. 15:19; 2 Cor. 12:12; Heb. 2:4).

The good news is that we, too, can have this powerful plus in our ministries today. Jesus promised this added power when He said, "You will receive power when the Holy Spirit comes on you" (Acts 1:8). Like those first disciples, we, too, must wait until we have been "clothed with power from on high" (Luke 24:49).

Two concepts central to our understanding of power ministry are "power encounter" and "truth encounter." A *power encounter* takes place when the power of God and the power of Satan come into direct conflict with one another. Anytime a demonic spirit must be overcome before the kingdom of God can advance calls for a power encounter (Matt. 12:28-29; Luke 11:20-22). This demonic presence could be ruling over an individual, a society, or a geographical area. Whatever the case, it must be challenged and defeated.

Elijah's challenging and defeating the prophets of Baal is a classic example of an Old Testament power encounter (1 Kings 18:19-40). Paul's challenging and defeating Elymas on the island of Cyprus is a New Testament example (Acts 13:6-12).

When the gospel is proclaimed in a place where its truth is being denied or opposed, a *truth encounter* occurs. Truth encounter goes hand in hand with power encounter. Power encounters challenge demonic spirits that are controlling individuals or areas where the gospel is advancing. Truth encounters challenge the false teachings that are holding a people in bondage. Truth encounter should always accompany power encounter. Once there has been a demonstration of God's power, there must always be a proclamation of Christ's gospel.

The combining of power encounter and truth encounter results in what John Wimber has called *power evangelism.*[2] The ministries of Jesus and the New Testament preachers are replete with examples of power evangelism. Jesus' ministry was often characterized by a combination of both proclamation and demonstration (Luke 24:19; Acts 1:1). A reading of the book of Acts reveals that same was true of the early church.

Ministry with a Biblical Precedent

Not only can power ministry be described as ministry with a powerful plus, it can also be described as ministry with a biblical precedent. The pattern for such ministry was set by Jesus Himself. Peter summarized Jesus' ministry in Acts 10:38: "How God anointed Jesus of Nazareth with the Holy Spirit and power, and how he went around doing good and healing all who were under the power of the devil, because God was with him."

Not only did Jesus Himself minister in the power of the Spirit, He appointed and taught His disciples to do the same (Mark 3:13-19; Luke 9:1-2; 10:1-2, 9). He promised them the same power He had (Acts 1:8), and, as a result of their receiving that power, they could expect the same results that He had had in His own ministry (John 14:12).

---

[2] John Wimber, *Power Evangelism,* (San Francisco, CA: Harper and Row Publishers, 1986).

The church was first empowered by the Spirit on the Day of Pentecost (Acts 2:1-4). As a result of this divine empowering, it went out and ministered in great power and with great results (Acts 2:41, 43, 47). Jesus set the pattern and the apostles and New Testament believers followed.

We, like those early disciples, must follow the pattern set by Jesus. We, too, must be filled with the Spirit. Further, we should expect to see God's power at work in our own ministries, healing the sick and delivering people from demonic bondage.

Ministry with a Mighty Potential

A third thing that we can say about power ministry is that it is ministry with a mighty potential. It has great potential in at least three areas of ministry:

1. Potential for bringing great blessing to the church. As the power of God is demonstrated in the congregation, the church is edified and built up (1 Cor. 14:24-26). Great blessings come as people are healed and set free from old habits and bondages. As the Word of God is preached with power, Christians are brought closer to God, and sinners are converted. As spiritual gifts are manifested in a spirit of love and humility, Jesus is exalted, God is glorified, and the church is blessed.

2. Potential for church planting and growth. Around the world missionary church planters can testify that few things open the hearts of a people to the gospel like a demonstration of God's compassionate power. When they see one of their own healed or set free, the people open their hearts wide to the message of Christ.

In Africa, in areas where a chief or ruling authority has resisted the planting of a new church, we have seen their minds changed as they witnessed a demonstration of God's healing power. Such a demonstration sets the stage for an effective presentation of the gospel. Once people have seen God's power, they are ready to listen to God's message.

3. *Potential for evangelizing resistant people groups.* A resistant people group is a tribe or clan of people who are very difficult to reach with the gospel. Today millions of these people live in an area of the world called the "10-40 Window." When missiologists talk about the 10-40 Window, they are talking about that part of the world that is located between the 10th and 40th parallels on a map of the world, extending from North Africa in the west to the eastern tip of Asia. The 10-40 Window contains most of the unreached peoples in the world.

Jesus has commissioned us to take the gospel to every one of these people (Mark 16:15, cf. Matt. 24:14). In these last days of time, the church is waking up to the fact that Jesus' original plan for reaching the world was, after all, the best. We can reach them only in the power of the Holy Spirit with signs following (Mark 16:15-16; Acts 1:8).

THE NEED FOR SPIRITUAL POWER IN MINISTRY

There are many reasons why the church is to be involved in power ministry today. Let's talk about three:

Because of the Needs Around Us

We need the Spirit's power manifested in our ministries because of the many needs of the people around us. Jesus is our example in ministry. It was after Jesus saw the great needs of those around Him that He sent His disciples out to do power ministry. Matthew notes that, when Jesus saw the people's needs, "he had compassion on them, because they were harassed and helpless, like sheep without a shepherd" (Matt. 9: 36). But what did He do about it?

The text says He did three things: First, He commanded His disciples to pray to the Lord of the harvest "to send out workers into his harvest field" (v. 38). Next, He called the Twelve "and gave them authority to drive out evil spirits and to heal every disease and sickness" (Matt. 10:1). Finally, He then sent them out to preach the kingdom of heaven and to "heal the sick, raise the dead, cleanse those who have leprosy, drive out demons" (vv. 7-8). Great human need called for power ministry.

As we look around us, we, too, see hurting people. These people include those possessed by evil spirits, AIDS victims, broken homes, and broken lives. Only the power of the Holy Spirit can break the chains that bind them and set them free. We, as God's people, must be His agents of hope and deliverance.

We, like Jesus, must minister to them in the power and anointing of the Holy Spirit with signs following.

Because of the Enemy Opposing Us

Another reason we need spiritual power in ministry is because we are opposed by a powerful enemy—Satan and his demonic hordes. Thankfully, Jesus has given to us power over "all the power of the enemy" (Luke 10:19). That power is the power of the Holy Spirit (Matt. 12:28).

Only a ministry anointed by the power of the Spirit can ever hope to defeat Satan. How foolish we would be to try to defeat him in our own power. We receive God's power by being baptized in the Holy Spirit, as were the early Christians. Then, as we walk in the Spirit, we can appropriate His power through faith, and we can defeat the enemy through the release of spiritual gifts according to the will of the Spirit (1 Cor. 12:8-10).

Because of the Challenge Facing Us

A third reason we need spiritual power in ministry is because of the enormous challenge facing us, the challenge of reaching the nations with the gospel before the soon coming of Christ (Matt. 24:14). How will we ever be able to accomplish such an awesome task? Only through the power of the Holy Spirit. Jesus has promised us all the power we need to get the job done (Acts 1:8).

HOW TO MINISTER IN POWER

The question now arises, "What must we do to be able to minister in the power and the anointing of the Holy Spirit?" There are at least three things we must do if we are to have such a ministry:

Acknowledge Our Need

First, we must acknowledge our need for God's power in our ministries. We must realize that, in ourselves, we are not adequate for the job. The needs around us are greater than all of our combined resources, and the power of Satan is greater than all of our combined power.

Paul must have been thinking on such things when he asked the question, "Who is equal to such a task?" (2 Cor. 2:16). He answered his own question:

> Not that we are competent in ourselves to claim anything for ourselves, but our competence comes from God. He has made us competent as ministers of a new covenant—not of the letter but of the Spirit; for the letter kills but the Spirit gives life. (2 Cor. 3:4-6)

Paul knew that, in himself, he was not able to do the work that God had given him. And yet, he also knew that he had been filled with the Spirit, and therefore, he was competent in God.

It is only as we realize our weakness, and humbly admit our need, that we are prepared to rely on His strength. The first step

to ministering in the power of the Holy Spirit is the realization and acknowledgment of our need.

Appropriate the Spirit's Help

Next, if we are to have a power ministry, we must learn to appropriate the Spirit's help. We do this by being filled with the Spirit. This was the pattern set by Jesus (Luke 4:18-19), and it is His clear plan for us today (Luke 24:49, Acts 1:8).

Further, we must also learn to appropriate the Spirit's aid by walking in humble submission to, and in constant communion with, Him. We must covet the Spirit's gifts (1 Cor. 12:31, 14:1) and be ready to respond to His directions and inner promptings. Only then will we be able to minister in spiritual power.

Act in Faith and Boldness

Finally, if we are to have an effective power ministry, we must learn to act in faith and boldness. As we discussed in the last chapter, the anointing of the Holy Spirit is appropriated through obedience and released through faith. Only those who are ready to act in bold faith will ever see signs and wonders accomplished in their ministries.

The needs around us are many. People are suffering and crying out for help. The task of world evangelization is great. How can we meet these challenges? We will successfully meet

them only in the power and anointing of the Holy Spirit. We must boldly preach Christ and expect supernatural signs to follow our ministries.

BIBLIOGRAPHY

Ervin, Howard M. *Spirit-Baptism, A Biblical Investigation.* Peabody, MA: Hendrickson Publishers, Inc., 1987.

Goodspeed, Edgar J. *The New Testament: An American Translation.* Chicago, IL: University of Chicago Press, 1948.

Harris, Ralph W. *Spoken by the Spirit: Documented Accounts of "Other Tongues" From Arabic to Zulu.* Springfield, MO: Gospel Publishing House, 1973.

_____. *The Complete Biblical Library, The New Testament Study Bible Galatians—Philemon.* Springfield, MO: World Library Press, Inc., 1991.

Horton, Stanley M. *What the Bible Says About the Holy Spirit.* Springfield, MO: Gospel Publishing House, 1976.

Martin, Ralph P. *The Worship of God.* Grand Rapids, MI: Wm. B. Eerdmans, 1982.

Miller, Denzil R. *Power Ministry: How to Minister in the Spirit's Power.* Springfield, MO: Africa's Hope, 2004.

_____. *Acts: The Spirit of God in Mission.* Springfield, MO: Africa's Hope, 2007.

Sorge, Bob. *Exploring Worship, A Practical Guide to Praise and Worship.* New Wilmington, PA: Son-Rise Publications, 1987.

Stamps, Don. *Full Life Study Bible, New International Version.* Springfield, MO: Life Publishers, 1992.

Williams, J. Rodman. *Renewal Theology: Systematic Theology from a Charismatic Perspective: Three Volumes in One.* Grand Rapids, MI: Zondervan Publishing House, 1992.

John Wimber and Keith Springer, *Power Evangelism.* San Francisco, CA: Harper and Row Publishers, 1986).

Womack, David A., ed. *Pentecostal Experience, the Writings of Donald Gee.* Springfield, MO: Gospel Publishing House, 1993.

Yonggi Cho, Paul. *Successful Home Cell Groups.* Bridge Logos Publishers, 1981.

OTHER BOOKS BY DENZIL R. MILLER

Power Ministry: How to Minister in the Spirit's Power
(available in English, French, Portuguese, Swahili,
Malagasy, Kinirwanda, and Chichewa)

*Empowered for Global Mission:
A Missionary Look at the Book of Acts*

From Azusa to Africa to the Nations
(available in English, French, Spanish, and Portuguese)

Acts: The Spirit of God in Mission

*The Kingdom and the Power: The Kingdom of God:
A Pentecostal Interpretation*

Teaching in the Spirit

Made in the USA
Monee, IL
11 January 2020